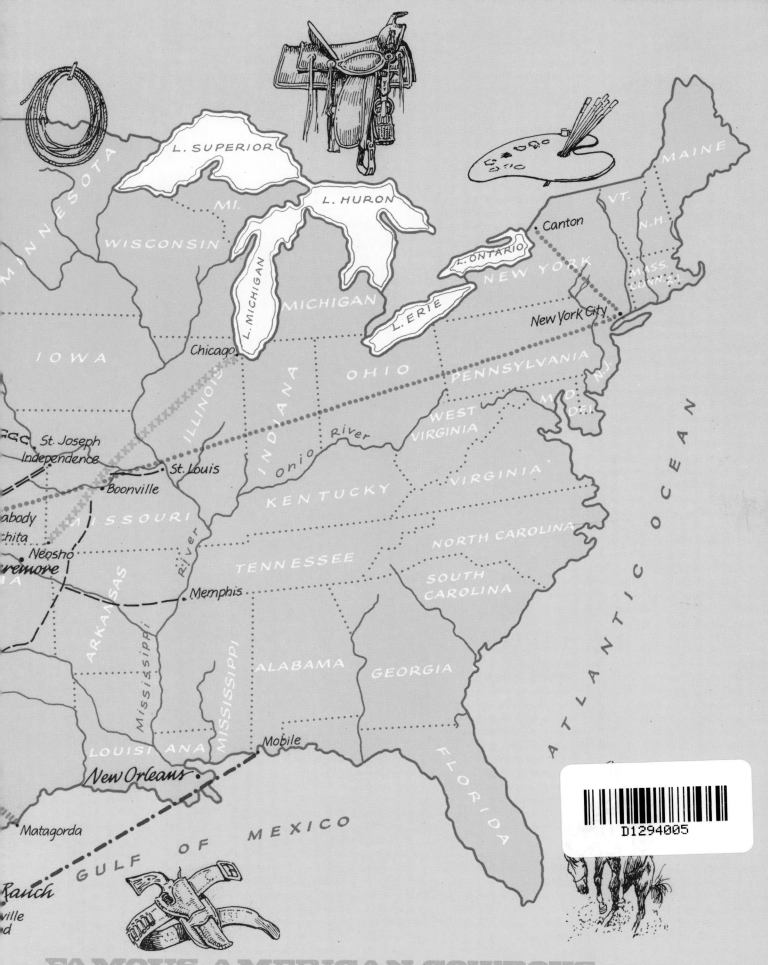

L. SUPERIOR

L. HURON

MI.

WISCONSIN

MINNESOTA

L. MICHIGAN

MICHIGAN

L. ONTARIO

NEW YORK

L. ERIE

MAINE

VT.

N.H.

MASS.
CONN. R.I.

Canton

New York City

IOWA

Chicago

INDIANA

OHIO

PENNSYLVANIA

MD. N.J.
DEL.

ILLINOIS

GC

St. Joseph

Independence

St. Louis

Ohio

River

WEST
VIRGINIA

VIRGINIA

Boonville

abody

MISSOURI

KENTUCKY

chita

Neosho

remore

ARKANSAS

River

TENNESSEE

NORTH CAROLINA

SOUTH
CAROLINA

Memphis

ATLANTIC OCEAN

Mississippi

Mississippi

ALABAMA

GEORGIA

LOUISIANA

Mobile

New Orleans

FLORIDA

Matagorda

GULF OF MEXICO

Ranch

ville

d

ATLANTIC OCEAN

FAMOUS AMERICAN COWBOYS

Famous American Cowboys

Famous American Cowboys

By BERN KEATING

Line Drawings by LORENCE BJORKLUND

RAND MᶜNALLY & COMPANY · CHICAGO · NEW YORK · SAN FRANCISCO

Library of Congress Cataloging in Publication Data

Keating Bern.
  FAMOUS AMERICAN COWBOYS

Includes index.
SUMMARY: Biographical sketches of nine cowboys including the cowboy showman, Will Rogers, Richard King, the cattle baron, and Frederic Remington, an artist whose drawings portrayed cowboy life.
    1. Cowboys—The West—Biography—Juvenile literature.
    2. The West—Biography—Juvenile literature. (1. Cowboys. 2. The West—Biography)
I. Bjorklund, Lorence F. II. Title.
F596.K37   978'.02'0922 (B)   (920)   77-5329
ISBN 0-528-82250-0
ISBN 0-528-80250-X lib. bdg.

Book Design by
MARIO PAGLIAI

FRONT COVER:
Cowboy Roping a Steer
by Charles Russell
FROM THE ORIGINAL OIL PAINTING AT
WOOLAROC MUSEUM, BARTLESVILLE, OKLAHOMA

Contents

Where Did the Cowboy Come From?

ON MARCH 14, 1519, somewhere along the coast of Mexico, Spanish sailors of the fleet under command of Hernando Cortés unloaded sixteen horses, the first in the historic New World. (The horse originated in North America but had become extinct there untold ages before.) These animals were from Andalusia in southern Spain, probably descended from the tough wild horses that once swarmed about the region, mixed with the beautiful Arabian stock brought from Africa by the conquering Moors. Escaping from Spanish herds, their descendants would go wild and run the plains of North America in vast herds that still exist in remote pockets of the far West.

Only two years later, while Cortés and his conquistadors were still fighting to subdue the Aztecs, Gregorio de Villalobos brought to Mexico a bull and six heifers of the Andalusian Longhorn breed, the vanguard of many herds brought from Spain to the New World.

To guard the rapidly growing numbers of longhorns, Spaniards enslaved a few Indians and branded them on the cheek as they branded their cattle to show ownership.

Cortés branded his cattle with a row of three crosses, the first recorded brand in the New World. Another conquistador named Coronado led a great cavalcade north from Mexico to conquer the mythical

11

cities in the deserts across the Rio Grande (or the Rio Bravo, as the Spaniards called it). Overburdened with slow-moving cattle, Coronado abandoned several hundred in northwestern Mexico. Only a generation later, explorers found thousands of cattle running wild in a country ideally suited for their breed. Ranchers quickly moved in and tried to make the wild cattle their own by planting a brand on their flanks. To brand the savage beasts, however, they had to catch them first, a hopeless job for a man on foot.

Spanish aristocrats had been so proud of their horsemanship that the very word for "gentleman"—*caballero*—meant horseman and implied noble birth. To keep Indian herdsmen working with domesticated flocks as slaves, they had been forbidden the noble's privilege of riding horses. Working the wild herds was a different matter, however, and the caballero was forced to mount his herdsmen. But he did not deign to call his herdsman a caballero just because he rode a horse. He called him a *vaquero*, or cowman. It is just a short step of translation from cowman to cowboy. In the far West, especially in the cattle country of California, English speakers did not bother to translate the word but deformed it into "buckaroo."

Everything about the American cowboy originated with the Mexican vaquero. Even the English words for most of the cowboy's equipment come from the vaquero—the *sombrero*, meaning a shade-maker; the lariat from the Mexican *la reata*, meaning the rope; chaps from *chaparajos* or *chaparreras*, probably having something to do with a dialect word for dense brush. If the cowboy got into trouble in town, he wound up in the calaboose from *calabozo*, meaning jail. The wild mustang was called in Spanish a *musteño*, meaning a runaway or stray. The supply of spare horses on a trail drive was a *remuda*, from the Spanish word for exchange or remount.

The practice of branding, the roundup, roping—all the features of life that set the cowboy apart from the herdsmen of any other region—were Mexican in origin and Andalusian before that.

Mexican vaqueros and their cattle entered what is now the American West by two routes—across the Rio Grande into Texas and by sea into California. The California vaquero, the true buckaroo, had a more flamboyant style of dress and horsemanship than the Texan, but his influence stayed on the far side of the Rocky Mountains. The Texas vaquero put his stamp on the Texas cowboy and from there the vaquero style spread across the vast Great Plains and into the northern ranges, even across the border into the Canadian prairie provinces.

The first Texans were farmers. What herding they did in the early nineteenth century was in the eastern style. Gradually newcomers saw a chance for quick profits in the huge herds of wild cattle roaming the grassy plains beyond the farmlands. They found the horses they needed among the mustangs running wild, the same reservoir of horseflesh the Plains Indians drew on for their war ponies and buffalo-hunting mounts. They found the manner of working wild cattle among the Mexican horsemen. A few immigrants, like Captain Richard King, made immense fortunes and acquired princely expanses of rangeland in those early days of rounding up wild cattle and horses.

The Civil War broke up the trade in beef, however, as the Union forces drew their strangling blockade tighter around the South. Even a cattle baron as powerful as Richard King turned to cotton trading for the duration of the war. Freed of the drainage to the slaughterhouse, the wild-running herds increased prodigiously. Confederate veterans returning to Texas after the war found the plains swarming with ownerless cattle, just as railroads pushing westward across the Mississippi as far as Kansas were opening the beef-hungry northern market.

Desperate for work, hundreds of war-weary veterans grabbed at the chance to round up the wild longhorns on open range, proclaim ownership by branding them, and drive them across 1200 miles of prairie through hostile Indian country to the railhead at Abilene, Kansas. The work was grindingly hard, the pay poor, the route dangerous, but there was never any lack of volunteers. For a little more than a decade, from 1867 to 1880, hundreds of thousands of heads of cattle went north, to be loaded into cattlecars for the slaughterhouses of Kansas City and Chicago, or to feed newcomers to the Plains as the native buffalo disappeared.

Beginning about 1875, Texans drove longhorns northward to Dodge City, Kansas, to restock the Great Plains, filling the vacuum left by the vanishing buffalo. Many Texans stayed in the North, forming the nucleus of the cowboy work force that handled cattle in the herds pouring into Nebraska, Colorado, Wyoming, Montana, and Oregon. There, the Texan longhorns ran into a stream of shorthorn cattle driven overland from the Pacific coast. Although admirably fitted to range life because of their ruggedness, longhorns were poor beef animals compared to the improved shorthorn breeds. Cattlemen of the North kept their longhorn cows, but replaced the bulls with shorthorns and were delighted to discover that cross-bred calves dressed out as superior beef like a shorthorn and stood up to hard range conditions like a longhorn.

Those Texas cattle and Texas cowboys came north by many trails. The most famous was certainly the Chisholm Trail from San Antonio to Abilene by way of Fort Worth, Texas, across Oklahoma, and through Wichita and Newton, Kansas. Oddly, the Jesse Chisholm who gave his name to the trail never drove a longhorn in his life. He was a half-breed Cherokee who drove a peddler's wagon bringing trade goods to the Indians. His oxen had plodded down a trail that perfectly suited the drivers of longhorn cattle and somehow his name stuck to it.

Romantics lament the end of the great days of cowboying, marking the decline about the time of the last trail drives late in the nineteenth century.

Ridiculous. Cattle do not round up and market themselves. The cowboy was and is very much part of the American West, and as long as grass grows on the vast plains and Americans love a juicy beefsteak, there are going to be cowboys to move those fine animals from the grasslands to the cattle cars. And no pickup truck or helicopter has yet been invented that can haze a cow and her calf out of a tangle of mesquite and into a corral as swiftly as a cowboy in his sombrero and chaps on a hard-muscled quarter horse, descendant of those Andalusian ponies that ran away from their Spanish owners four centuries ago.

To this day the cowboy wears a uniform to show he takes pride in his way of life. Not everybody who affects a broad-brimmed hat and high-heeled boots is a cowboy, of course, but it is a safe bet that every cowboy wears a western-style hat and cowboy boots. In fact, a cowboy rarely takes off his hat. One rancher, quoted by a historian at the University of Oklahoma, indicated why cowboys are attached to their headgear.

They shade your eyes, keep the rain from running down your neck, and keep you from being beaten to death with hailstones. They make the best eyeshades in the world—for reading, playing poker, or what have you. These high-school kids who go without hats puzzle me. I wonder why they don't protect their brains, if they have any—why they wear slickers in the rain, but no hats. They go out in these convertibles and rain runs down their necks so they have to sit in it. I'd feel like a baby that needs to be changed.

Those reasons for wearing the cowboy hat are good reasons, but almost certainly not the real reason. The real reason is to proudly advertise to the world that the wearer is a cowboy.

The Texas Cattle Baron

AMONG THE CATTLEMEN who first rounded up the wild Spanish cattle from the open range of Texas, branded them, and built a fortune out of hard work and shrewd business sense were some of the great names of western history. Charles Goodnight was a Texas Ranger before ranching in the Panhandle and opening a new trail to supply beef to army forts and Indian reservations in New Mexico. Shanghai Pierce rounded up and shipped tens of thousands of longhorns, gathered an immense fortune, and made an effort to look and live like the poorest of his vaqueros. (He was reputed to have died with a firm grasp on the first dollar he ever made.) Though he carried huge sums of money about the bandit-infested prairie, Shanghai Pierce never carried a weapon on the theory that the most bloodthirsty robber would not kill an unarmed man. Shaky as the theory seems, it worked, for he died an old man of natural causes.

The most famous and most successful of the great cattle barons of Texas was not a cowboy, not even a westerner, but a steamboat pilot from the East.

Richard King was born in New York City. Little is known of his parents. He may have been the child of Irish immigrants, for his speech had an Irish turn of phrase. When he was eleven years old, he ran away from a jeweler's workshop where he was an apprentice and stowed away

18

on a ship bound for Mobile, Alabama. Discovered early in the voyage, he talked his way into a job as cabin boy. The ship's captain taught him to read and write and to do the arithmetic necessary for navigation. By the time he was nineteen, he had a pilot's license to navigate steamboats on the rivers along the Florida Panhandle coast of the Gulf of Mexico. There he met a Quaker named Mifflin Kenedy, an older and better educated steamboat pilot. Captain Kenedy signed up with the U. S. Army Engineers to supply by steamboat the troops of General Zachary Taylor camped on the Rio Grande and preparing for a war with Mexico. He took Richard King with him as pilot of the steamboat *Corvette*.

During the Mexican War, Captain King moved troops and supplies up and down the river from the mouth as far upstream as Camargo, on the Mexican side. When the war ended in November, 1847, he had not suffered an accident, an unheard-of record on that treacherous river.

He and Captain Kenedy and a succession of business partners had a monopoly on steamboating on the Rio Grande. During the next twenty-four years they operated twenty-six boats.

In April, 1852, Captain King rode overland across the strip between the Nueces River and the Rio Grande to attend the state fair at Corpus Christi. Camping on Santa Gertrudis Creek, he was struck by the abundance of good fresh water in a sea of grass swarming with unbranded wild cattle.

The only drawback was that bandits, rustlers, and hostile Indians had spotted the same opportunity and were not above mixing a few branded cattle in with the unbranded mavericks they rounded up. In that chaotic day, a brand meant nothing unless the rancher had some tough and heavily armed vaqueros to protect it.

Captain King showed the kind of business sense that was to make him the undisputed first among the Texas cattle barons. For two cents an acre, he bought 15,500 acres of the grassland about forty-five miles southwest of Corpus Christi, but only after going into partnership with Gideon K. "Legs" Lewis, who very conveniently was captain of a company of Texas Rangers. While Captain Lewis's hard-boiled Rangers patrolled the countryside, sweeping it clear of rustlers, Captain King built dams on small creeks to make ponds that could water a thousand head of cattle at a time.

From the beginning, though he never learned to speak good Spanish, Captain King depended heavily on Mexican vaqueros for his work force. When the Ranger company disbanded, he used his Mexican connections as a spy network to report any strangers that might threaten his herds. He built a blockhouse and set up a loaded cannon. As foremen for his Mexican riders, he hired vaqueros with reputations as tough *hombres,* and let the word leak out that his ranch was an armed camp and his cowboys ready for any kind of fight. As a consequence, he didn't have any trouble, for bandits wisely hit weaker settlements.

When a drouth hit the area, instead of cutting down his herds as other ranchers were doing, he bought thousands of new cattle at low prices, risking the savings of a lifetime of steamboating on the chance the drouth would soon end. He bought the entire herd of one Mexican village. Because there was no reason for the village to exist without its cattle, he moved the whole population to the fortified strong point at Santa Gertrudis and signed them on as ranch hands. He won his bet on the weather when heavy rains came.

His partner Lewis was killed in a private quarrel, but Captain King thought he was strong enough to go it alone, with the help of the U. S. Army border guard, of course. He had not counted on the stupidity of the general commanding the U. S. Army on that frontier.

Just as Mexico declared a six-mile-wide belt along the Rio Grande free of customs inspection, creating a vacuum of authority sure to suck in every smuggler, rustler, and cutthroat in Mexico and Texas, General David E. Twiggs withdrew all army troops.

"There is not, nor ever has been, any danger of the Mexicans crossing on our side of the river to plunder or disturb its inhabitants," said the supremely mistaken general.

However, bandits ran wild in the Nueces Strip between the Nueces and the Rio Grande, skinning cattle, raiding ranches, looting, and killing.

Among them, the undisputed leader was Juan Nepomuceno Cortinas, a red-haired and fair-skinned Mexican given to the wearing of military dress. He had been born in Texas to a rich family.

Despite his high-born background he never learned to read and write, but he was a crack shot and a recklessly courageous leader of his own people. Defending his own ranch, he wiped out a band of hostile Indians, probably the very last of the once-powerful tribe of Karankawas.

On July 13, 1859, he was sharing coffee with some of his cronies at a cafe in Brownsville, Texas. The town marshall arrived to arrest a drunken Mexican who had once been Juan's servant. The city marshall slapped his Mexican prisoner about and Cortinas asked him to be more polite. The marshall made the grave mistake of underrating the red-haired Mexican and abused him verbally. Cortinas shot him through the shoulder, loaded the drunken ex-servant behind him on his horse, and dashed out of town.

News of his defense of a simple Mexican spread like a prairie fire. Recruits poured into his rancho (on the Texas side of the river) offering to join forces against the *gringos*. On September 28, 1859, Cortinas and a hundred men captured Brownsville, killed five men, freed prisoners from the city jail, and threw the region as far as King's ranch into an uproar.

Brownsville merchants sent a punitive force against the Cortinas ranch. The patrol was made up of sixty Mexican-Americans, twenty gringos, and a company of Mexican Army infantry lent by authorities across the border in an extraordinary gesture of friendship. Cortinas bushwhacked the column and drove them back in disorder, capturing the two cannon they had brought along.

After his victory at the ranch, Cortinas rampaged about the countryside, sowing anarchy and terror. A company of Texas Rangers under Captain W. G. Tobin arrived to police the country, but they appear to have been a band of lawless toughs led by an incompetent. They added nothing to the generally glorious history of the Texas Rangers. On the first Ranger march against the bandit chieftain, Cortinas trounced them soundly, killing three Rangers. He gained tremendous prestige among Mexicans for whipping not just Texans, but actual Texas Rangers.

Upstate the governor called back to service a famed Ranger veteran, John Ford, known as Rip Ford. He started with only eight men but on his sweep southward picked up a full company of heavily-armed recruits. His reputation as a hard-fighting Ranger during the Mexican War put heart into the ranchers and townfolk of the Nueces Strip when they heard he was on the way.

The U. S. Army also belatedly decided it had business after all in the Nueces country. One hundred regulars under Major Samuel Heintzelman at Fort Brown replaced the Mexican soldiers so graciously lent by the Republic to prevent the sack of Brownsville. Beefed up by Tobin's Rangers, the regulars attacked Cortinas at a crude fort in the brush and drove him off. He did not act like a defeated leader, however, for he ravaged the countryside up the Rio Grande, pillaging Rio Grande City, Texas, on Christmas Day, 1859.

Unknown to Cortinas, a real Ranger leader had arrived on the scene. Ford's company had arrived too late for Major Heintzelman's first battle, but the two joined forces to bring on another and more decisive battle upstream. Marching ahead, the Rangers encountered the bandit army first and clashed with Cortinas near Laredo. Though heavily outnumbered, the Rangers shattered a bandit charge and drove the force across the river into Mexico before the army reinforcements could arrive on the scene.

Encouraged by the battle, the captain of one of the steamboats owned by Captain King (and his several partners) ventured a trip on the river to carry $60,000 in gold from Rio Grande City to Brownsville. Cortinas openly built a fort at a sharp bend in the river and manned it with a bandit force to capture the steamboat when it slowed for the bend.

The steamboat captain had taken aboard the two cannon captured from Cortinas at Laredo, and Captain Ford crossed a large band of Rangers into Mexico. When the battle opened, a storm of grapeshot from the cannon forced the bandits to huddle out of sight behind their fort while the Rangers circled around the fort and took them from the rear.

The bandits fled, Cortinas the last to leave the field after emptying his pistol at the Rangers. Captain King's steamboat was saved and the company resumed full service on the river.

Two years later during the Civil War, Cortinas tried to resume his banditry, but he ran into a band of irregular cavalry, much like a Ranger company, made up of Chicanos and led by a gallant soldier named Captain Santos Benavides. The Mexican-American cavalrymen soundly thrashed Cortinas and chased him across the river for the duration of the war.

The outbreak of war in 1861 virtually killed the cattle market. Rip Ford at the head of a scratched-together Texas force seized all the Union strong points on the Rio Grande, however, and thus opened a new trade for Captain King. The port of Bagdad just across the Rio Grande in Mexico became a major Confederate outlet for trade with the world after the Union navy blockaded all the ports within the southern states. Captain King's Santa Gertrudis ranch became the main warehouse for transport of cotton from the farmlands farther north and east to the buyers from British and French cotton mills across the river in Mexico.

Confederate leaders in far-off Richmond never got through their heads the tremendous importance of their lands west of the Mississippi River. They stripped the Rio Grande of its defenses to beef up their forces farther north, so that the mouth of the Rio Grande fell easily to a Union invasion force. The fleeing Confederates passed through the King ranch. The only effective Confederate force left in the Nueces Strip was the Chicano cavalry company of Captain Benavides, who took over the transport of cotton across the river far upstream from the Union force. The cotton went by road down the Mexican bank to Bagdad. Unable to operate against Benavides in the desert upriver, the Union general decided to choke off the cotton trade by attacking the King ranch. He sent sixty soldiers against Santa Gertrudis. Captain King got word immediately through his Chicano spy network and left the ranch in charge of his foreman Francisco Alvarado.

At dawn, Union soldiers fired into the ranch house. Alvarado went to the porch to shout. "Don't fire on this house. There is a family here."

He fell dead with a bullet through the heart. The troops plundered the ranch before leaving. It happened to be Christmas Eve.

As often happens, Ford had been so brilliant a soldier in the field that he was promoted to a desk job where his combat talents were wasted.

After the fall of Brownsville to the Union army, however, the governor of Texas called him back into field service. He drove the Union forces back to a bare toehold at the mouth of the river, recaptured Captain King's steamboats, set up a chain of relay stations between Brownsville and Santa Gertrudis, and reopened a brisk cotton trade. Though the Confederacy collapsed in April, 1865, and the struggle was officially over, Ford had not received the word and on May 13, 1865, he routed a Union force in the last battle of the war.

Captain King fled to Matamoros in Mexico, just across the river from Brownsville. At a meeting with victorious Union officials, he agreed to return to Texas and help restore normal government and commerce.

Captain King had profited handsomely from the cotton trade during the war. He foresaw the death of steamboating as railroads expanded and turned his attention almost entirely to ranching. He profited from the ownerless cattle delivered to him without cost by the big blizzard during the winter of 1863–1864. This terrible storm had driven immense numbers of cattle from the north, across the unfenced range, to pile up on the Gulf of Mexico coast.

Even before the invention of barbed wire, Captain King began closing in his lands with fences, a shocking expense to old-fashioned ranchers who preferred to let their cattle run free to graze any land they chose till roundup time.

Those cattle running free, most of them unbranded because the cowboys had been off to war, again created an irresistible temptation to bandits. When Cortinas returned this time, he was a brigadier general in the Mexican army. He organized banditry as a kind of Mexican mafia, stocked four of his ranches with stolen Texas cattle, and shipped thousands more from Bagdad to Havana to feed the Spanish army.

The King ranch lost approximately fifty-four thousand head despite the fences and armed patrols. Captain King rode with a double-barrelled shotgun loaded with buckshot (he never trusted a six-shooter) and he mounted two cannon at the ranch. He bought thirty rifles and hired gunmen to strengthen his vaquero force.

Almost as dangerous as the bandit hordes were vigilante companies who hanged Mexicans at random with no evidence of guilt and took revenge on gringo enemies under the guise of enforcing the law. Ranchers fled the Nueces Strip, and it was fast reverting to desert.

In June, 1875, a Ranger company under Captain Leander McNelly arrived at the King ranch with the sole mission of cleaning out the bandits. Captain King replaced their horses with fresh mounts and promised them all-out support.

Almost immediately, Captain McNelly wiped out a bandit gang and recovered a stolen herd just outside Brownsville. His Rangers campaigned along the Rio Grande and finally crossed the river in pursuit of a stolen herd. In a comic opera war with a bandit force that claimed to be part of the Mexican National Guard—which indeed they may have been since Cortinas the bandit chief was also an army officer—Captain McNelly forced the Mexicans to return some of the stolen cattle. Among them were thirty-five wearing the King Ranch brand.

When Porfirio Diaz seized power in Mexico, he kicked Cortinas upstairs to an honorary position in Mexico City, which was really a form of house arrest. On his side of the river, the Mexican dictator established the *Rurales*, patrols of mounted Federal police much like the Texas Rangers. Because of ruthless executions of bandits by Rurales and Rangers, and with Cortinas off the scene, the region returned to comparative peace.

An example of the new tasks facing the Nueces country: Captain King hired several of McNelly's Rangers as cowhands to help round up the tens of thousands of cattle and move them 1,100 miles north to the railroad at Abilene, Kansas. With his profits, Captain King steadily acquired more land. At his death in 1885 his ranch covered almost 1,000 square miles and was 91 percent as large as the entire state of Rhode Island. No other American cattle baron ever ruled over so vast a region. And so wisely had the steamboat captain planned ahead that his cattle kingdom exists intact today.

The Working Cowboy

THOUGH THE VAST unbranded herds wandering the open range of Texas after the Civil War gave equal opportunity for all to make a fortune, as always a lucky and hard-driving few made all the money and the rest did the dirty work. Intelligence was not necessarily the difference between the fate of the cattle baron and the working cowboy. Witness the autobiography of Charles A. Siringo, a delightful book showing the keen intelligence and sense of humor of a Texan who worked cattle most of his young years but never owned an acre of range land.

Despite his Spanish-looking name, Charles Siringo was born in 1856 of an Italian father and an Irish mother on the Matagorda Peninsula of Texas on the Gulf of Mexico coast. During the Civil War, Texans rounded up all the cattle on the coast and drove them to the interior to keep them out of Union hands. There the cattle became wild again and multiplied astronomically until the day the war ended and the cowboys came back from army service to round them up and brand them for their bosses.

He stayed in St. Louis awhile and then started rambling. He was adopted by a childless couple in New Orleans, but stabbed a schoolmate, thought it advisable to go back to St. Louis, and stowed away on a steamboat. He was scalded when the steamboat's engine blew up. After recovering from his burns, he began looking for his family. When he couldn't locate them, Siringo went back to his adopted parents in New Orleans. He attended school for a few more months, until the urge to wander came on him and he again stowed away, on a boat headed for Indianola, Texas, a major port that has since blown away in a hurricane.

Siringo tried farming but gave it up and signed on as a cowhand for Shanghai Pierce, the shrewd and notoriously stingy cattle baron. His first job was to help round up 1,100 longhorns sold to a blacksmith from Kansas who—with a band of his friends, all inexperienced in the ways of Texas cattle—planned to drive them home. The whole herd got away from the greenhorns and wandered back to their home range, where Shanghai had the pleasure of rounding them up and selling them a second time.

Shanghai taught his cowboys a technique of roping, branding, and earmarking unbranded cattle, known as mavericks, and releasing them in the midst of his tame herd. The wild creatures usually stayed on, but if they persisted in rambling Shanghai had their eyelids sewn shut till they accepted life in the Pierce herd.

Like most of the other cowboys, Siringo took note of how easy it was to acquire cattle at that time and place, so he began carrying a straight iron to plant his own brand on an occasional stray. He says he felt like a cattle king with so many cattle rambling about bearing his brand, but he realized on second thought that without constant guarding those cattle belonged to the first rustler or even the first cattle baron like Pierce who planted a new brand on his cow.

At settling time, Pierce's bookkeeper laid out 300 silver dollars, then raked back $299.25 for loans and expenses, leaving Siringo a profit of seventy-five cents for the season's hard work.

Siringo then worked at a slaughterhouse where cattle were killed for their hides and tallow, the beef going to feed hogs. He skinned as many as two hundred cattle a day and made public mention that not all the hides carried the operator's brand. Perhaps that is why he was transferred to caring for a herd of horses.

As Siringo put it, "There were about two hundred head of those and they were scattered in two hundred and fifty different places. . . ."

He continued to brand the odd maverick but with little hope of ever seeing it again. According to the custom of the day, he skinned any cattle he found dead. Siringo also slyly hints that he actually helped some of

those maverick cattle to be dead for the sake of skinning them.

Overgrazing and a savage winter lent the skinners a hand, as cattle froze by the thousands. Siringo said that after a sleet storm in one spot near the Matagorda Bay shore he could have walked for miles on cattle corpses without touching the ground.

In 1874, near the dying days of the great trail drives, he signed up for thirty-five dollars a month, living expenses on the trail, and a railroad ticket home. The herd stampeded. Siringo and his comrades rounded up all but a hundred out of the original 1,100—a much better record than the Kansas greenhorns registered—and they did not even lose much on the strays, for the original owner, unlike the ruthless Shanghai Pierce, bought them back at half-price on the assumption they would wander back to rejoin their home herd.

On the trail, Siringo fell out with the trail boss. He was a crack broncobuster, so whenever he gentled a wild horse the boss assigned it to a less skilled horseman and gave Siringo another brute to pacify. Worn out and saddle sore, Siringo quit.

Born on the Gulf shore and reared on the Mississippi River, Siringo was no stranger to navigation, so he turned to the sea for a living. He traded a rickety horse to an Englishman for a spavined schooner—it is hard to say who skinned whom in the deal, though Siringo congratulated himself, even years later, on his sharp practice. During this brief nautical interlude, the cowboy ran melons and oysters up and down the Gulf coast before he got the idea of sailing up the Colorado River (the Texas stream of that name emptying into the Gulf at Matagorda) to trade trinkets with black farmers along its banks. He hired a drayman with rollers to slide his schooner across a sand bar blocking the river mouth and loaded the ship with trade goods and tobacco.

Discouraged after his hired hand ran off with the stores, Siringo sold the schooner as it stood high and dry on the sandbar to the drayman for twenty-five dollars and went back to what he called "the hurricane deck of a Spanish pony."

Siringo is perhaps understandably vague about some events. In some shadowy encounter the heavy bullet of a dragoon pistol went through his kneecap and was dug out from the back of his leg. A shattered kneecap is almost invariably a crippling accident, but Siringo suffered no ill effects. Astoundingly, he was shot again through the same knee and still walked about like a natural man.

He goes into more detail about an adventure on Salt Fork during a trail drive. A flash flood cut the herd and its drivers off from the chuck wagon and their food supply. For seven days, they lived on fresh beef as the rain continued to pelt down. A cowboy scouted around and found a camp of soldiers across a swollen creek. The hungry drivers shouted across the swiftly flowing waters, begging for civilized food. The soldiers hurled some biscuits across the stream (a bad indication of the weight and edibility of Army fare) and agreed to give more food if the cowboys could get it across the stream.

Siringo was the best swimmer, so he made the crossing. He swam back pushing a washtub full of flour, salt, and coffee.

Back at camp, the famished cowboys made a kind of bread by rolling dough around a stick and holding it over a fire.

"Some of them sat up all night eating, trying to make up for lost time," Siringo reports.

At Wichita, Kansas, the end of the line, the trail boss paid off the hands and they went into town for a bit of fun. Like many another cowboy, within three days Siringo had blown every penny he had made during months on the trail.

On his way home, he built a shanty with the idea of wintering on the prairie. As he was preparing to move in, he heard an ominous crackling and wheeled about to see his intended house go up in flames, burning his blankets and overcoat and setting the prairie ablaze. Undaunted, he dug a cave in a riverbank, built a fire inside, and settled down for a rest. A steer fell through the roof, pinned him against the hot coals, and bruised him mercilessly as it thrashed about trying to escape.

Again, Siringo becomes coy about his perhaps disreputable adventures. *Well, Patient Reader, I will now drop the curtain for a while. Just suffice it to say I had a tough time of it during the rest of the winter and came out carrying two bullet wounds.*

Nothing tells better the nature of the rootless cowboy than Siringo's next move. He started for Kiowa, Kansas, but ran into a head wind that annoyed him, so he turned the horse's head and started for Texas instead.

He reports that from a camp at the edge of the Staked Plain (nobody knows why this part of west Texas and east New Mexico carries

this curious name) he watched one herd of buffalo three miles wide take three days and nights to cross the Canadian River.

While trying to catch up with a trail herd that had a head start, he and a comrade saw a large band of Indians in the distance. Because they were low on food, they debated asking the Indians for a handout, a common practice on the frontier. They rode toward the band, but something did not feel right, so they turned aside at the last moment. At the next settlement they discovered that the Indians were a war party that had been ravaging the countryside, burning cabins and killing settlers.

Siringo had several encounters with Billy the Kid. At a ranch north of Abilene, Texas, Billy and his gang turned up with a herd of ponies stolen in New Mexico. Later, at a party on the Maxwell ranch in New Mexico, Siringo escorted a girl to the door of her room. She acted strangely and would not open the door till he left. He later discovered that Billy the Kid was hiding from the law on the other side of the door. The outlaw was killed at the Maxwell ranch shortly after.

After suffering several accidents because of his heavy drinking, Siringo gave up whiskey. Near what is now Clarendon, Texas, he seems to have joined a congregation that had a lone church on the prairie, the only building in sight. Some enterprising businessmen built a saloon at the same site and Siringo, the reformed drinker, joined the mob of religious folk who drove away the purveyors of whiskey with threats of gunfire. Apparently the pious congregation considered murder a small price to pay for preventing the heinous sin of selling booze. Certainly, the tone of Siringo's story indicates he felt noble about driving away the would-be bartenders at the point of a gun.

The thin line between an honest cowboy and a rustler shows in Siringo's wry report on his style of living near White Oaks Ranch in the winter of 1880.

The grub we ate wasn't very expensive as we stole all of our meat, and shared with our honest neighbors, who thought it a great sin to kill other people's cattle. You see, Bob and I still clung to the old Texas style, which is, never kill one of your own beeves when you can get somebody else's.

Near Toyah, Texas, he entered a turkey shoot. The target was a turkey in an iron box, with only its head visible. Siringo says he clipped off two heads with two shots and was eliminated from the competition because he was too good and threatened to bankrupt the game's operator.

Perhaps his most horrendous adventure began in Colorado City where a smallpox epidemic was raging. He left town to escape the disease but became ill on the trail. He asked settlers along the road for shelter, but they slammed the door in his pustule-covered face, forcing him to sleep in the snow for eight nights. Somehow he lived through the illness that carried off almost half of its victims, even though his nights in the open themselves were almost enough to kill a well man.

Near the Rio Grande thieves ran off with both of his ponies. He dickered with a Mexican to rent a pony so he could chase the thieves across the river into Mexico. Certain that Siringo would never come back alive, the pony's owner insisted that the cowboy deposit the entire value of the pony so he would not suffer a loss through Siringo's death.

Siringo followed the trail about thirty-five miles into Mexico and found his ponies tied to a bush while the thieves were off hunting in the brush. He stole his ponies back and raced for the river, leaving the thieves to get out of the desert as best they could afoot.

Siringo moved to Caldwell, Kansas, and became a merchant. He was too restless for such a quiet life, however, and soon became a range detective, tracking down cattle thieves, a job he held for many years. He died in Hollywood, California, in 1928, leaving behind several books about his adventures. Though it must be admitted many ranchers disapproved of his books and thought Siringo was a tramp, his works remain some of the best western reading in the library.

The Cattle Baron, Northern Style

EARLY IN THE nineteenth century cattlemen moved to the High Plains to provide beef for emigrants headed for California and Oregon and for miners and U. S. Army frontier soldiers. The herds were small, however, compared to the vast wild herds wandering over Texas. After the Civil War, as railroads reached the region, cattle began to pour into the states of Colorado, Kansas, Nebraska, Wyoming, the Dakotas, Montana, and eastern Oregon. As early as 1866, Nelson Story brought the first herd of Texas longhorns to Montana.

Writers of lurid adventure stories excited the imagination of the East and Europe with stories of the great riches to be won in the cattle country. Fearing the competition of western beef with British herds, the English sent a Royal Commission to investigate. They reported that the West teemed with cattle, that Texas was a vast natural nursery, that open range was free for the taking. British investors clamored for a piece of the western action. French and Irish aristocrats went West to seek adventure while swelling their bankrolls.

Among the most avid investors were Scottish capitalists who banded together in syndicates to buy cattle and turn them loose on the range. Naturally, they sent trusted representatives to look after their interests.

Among the foreigners who flocked to the West after the Civil War

OVERLEAF:
Men of the Open Range
by Charles M. Russell
MACKAY COLLECTION, COURTESY MONTANA HISTORICAL SOCIETY

was John Clay, a Scotsman representing a Scottish syndicate. He arrived in 1880 and soon supervised a complex of ranches in Wyoming, Montana, and the Dakotas.

The holdings look impressive at first glance, but in truth the companies owned only narrow strips along watercourses and grazed their cattle on government land open to everybody. Homesteaders began to trickle into the region to take the 160 acres guaranteed them by the Homestead Act of 1862. Free use of the range by the big absentee landlords was fading. Then disaster struck in the winter of 1886–1887 when savage blizzards killed vast numbers of cattle.

As big investors failed and withdrew from the scene, homesteaders flocked in and occupied their lands. They built their small herds by mavericking, a custom traditional in the West since early days in Texas by which any cowboy could brand and claim any stray unbranded cattle on public lands. The big ranchers did not like the custom—or at least they did not like having small homesteaders using the custom to take cattle that could have come only from the big herds.

That big cattlemen were themselves not finicky about ownership of cattle is proved by an old chestnut told all over the West. According to the story, a rancher invited a neighboring cattleman to a dinner featuring a dish he had never tasted before. When the dinner was over, a simple steak and potato meal like ten thousand he had eaten before, the guest asked in bewilderment what was the exotic dish he supposedly had never tasted.

"It was beef from your own cattle."

Everywhere in the West during the days before fences closed in the open range, ranchers considered it stupid to kill one of their own beeves when a neighbor's was handy. But the big ranchers thought the pleasant custom of mavericking was too good for the common people. They formed the Wyoming Stock Growers Association with John Clay as president to work together against the small ranchers. Under the Maverick Law, which made every unbranded animal the property of the Association, their officers confiscated 16,306 cattle from homesteaders and sold them without giving the owners a hearing or trial.

Local newspapers sided with the little people in spite of the economic power of the big companies. The Stock Growers Association had the gall to order the editor of the *Cheyenne Sun* "to appear before the executive committee" at once to explain a hostile editorial. The foreign ranchers had neglected to read the amendment of the U. S. Constitution guaranteeing freedom of the press and they had further failed to gauge the touchiness of American journalists.

The rival *Cheyenne Leader*, outraged at the high-handed manner of the Association officers, raged against the un-American effort to suppress civil liberties and force "the weaker elements to immigrate or crawl, cowed and subdued, to the feet of the fierce and implacable oligarchy."

The big ranchers countered that they could not get a cattle thief convicted in court because juries were on the side of the little against the big. The exasperated representatives of big money took the law into their own hands and planned to drive out the homesteaders with professional gun fighters in the classic manner made familiar to millions by Grade B western movies and TV thrillers. This was to be the climax of the Johnson County War. The gunmen were called range detectives, but their role was to spread terror. The most famous and feared was Tom Horn, who lived with Clay as a house guest.

First to feel their wrath were a mild-mannered but stubborn store keeper named James Averill and a neighbor named Ella Watson, also known as Cattle Kate. She may have been Averill's wife, but concealed their relationship so she could also claim a 160-acre homestead on the Sweetwater range, thus doubling their holdings. Averill persisted in writing angry letters to the newspapers denouncing the big cattle operators.

A vigilante band, possibly led by one of the big ranchers himself, rounded up the pair and hanged them from the same tree, claiming the woman had eighty stolen cattle on her place. They didn't even bother to justify the hanging of Averill, for he possessed no cattle at all.

Far from being scared by the hangings, the small settlers, especially those in Wyoming's Johnson County up north near the Montana border, became enraged. When two homesteaders were shot down from ambush, the settlers rebelled against the state-backed Association and formed their own Northern Wyoming Farmers' and Stock Growers' Association. They announced that any stray cattle found in their part of the world henceforth belonged to their association and not to the Cheyenne-based rich man's club, as the Maverick Law provided.

Four men rode up to the small ranch of Thomas Waggoner, a hard-working German farmer,, and showed him a warrant for his arrest. He went with them quietly. Eight days later, searchers found his body hanging over the rim of a dry gulch. A foreman for one of the large ranches,

Tom Smith freely admitted leading the vigilantes and said Waggoner was a horse thief who did not deserve a fair trial.

On the Powder River, four vigilantes crept up to a shack where two Johnson County men, Nate Champion and Ross Gilbertson, were sleeping. Champion awakened as they charged the door, jerked his revolver out from under the blankets, and got off six shots, hitting several of the gunmen. The vigilantes fled, leaving behind their overcoats, bedding, a brand-new Winchester rifle, and most astonishing of all, their horses, which implies a very severe fright indeed, for cowboys would rather ride a tiger bareback than go afoot. The two Johnson County men identified the rifle as belonging to an Association ruffian. Champion's success in running off the would-be assassins made Johnson County bolder.

The big cattlemen decided to go all out. They sent Tom Smith to Texas where he hired a band of twenty-two professional gunmen as a private army to wipe out resistance in Johnson County in a full-scale military campaign. The plan was to isolate Johnson County by cutting telegraph wires, to kill the sheriff and marshall of the county seat at Buffalo with the first two shots of the war, then proceed to wipe out seventy so-called rustlers on a blacklist provided by Association detectives. To pay the $5 daily wage plus a $50 bonus for every rustler killed and other expenses, 100 members of the Association put up $1,000 each.

John Clay left for Europe, a curious but canny thing for the Association's leader to do.

Bolder than their president, nineteen Association members joined the hired bravos.

On April 6, 1892, the small army unloaded from a train at Casper, Wyoming. They checked the telegraph and were pleased to discover that Buffalo had been cut off.

From that point on, the dangerous but silly game became a fiasco. Horses ran away, forcing long delays while riders rounded them up. An unseasonable snowstorm held up the vigilante army. A scout reported that he had found a band of rustlers at a cabin only 15 miles away. An experienced range detective pleaded with the force not to be led astray but to plow ahead for the main target at Buffalo. The gunmen could not pass up the chance for a little fun on the side, however, and they headed through the snowstorm for the cabin where Nate Champion and Nick Ray were staying.

Nick Ray walked out the door and was shot down by a sniper. The redoubtable Nate Champion, the same Nate who had routed the band of would-be assassins in an earlier attack, pulled his comrade back through the door. For the rest of that long day, Nate alone stood off the vigilantes and calmly wrote a record of the battle in a notebook.

He reported seeing two strangers ride by and escape pursuit by members of the Texas band.

Toward nightfall he wrote, *Well, they have just got through shelling the house like hail. I heard them splitting wood. I guess they are going to fire the house tonight. I think I will make a break when night comes, if alive. Shooting again. It's not night yet. The house is all fired. Goodbye, boys, if I never see you again.*

He fled from the burning cabin, but fell within a few steps, riddled by bullets.

Their all day battle with the lone and courageous cowboy Champion cost the gunmen dearly, for the two passersby who had escaped pursuit alarmed Buffalo. The sheriff raised a powerful posse and Paul Reveres raced through the Wyoming countryside, calling out the small farmers and ranchers of outraged Johnson County.

When the vigilante scouts warned that a powerful band of armed ranchers was approaching from Buffalo, the Association band retreated in haste to the TA Ranch. The rest of that day was spent fortifying the ranch house with heavy timbers, trenches, and earthworks, a strange activity for a band that had planned to sweep unopposed through the land, sowing terror. The first party that attacked the ranch was scarcely as strong as the Texas "army" and made no pretense of being made up of professional killers, but they scared the Association thugs into cowering behind their fortifications. The Johnson County force quickly grew with reinforcements, till virtually every able-bodied man was on hand and the women had set up a kitchen to keep them well fed and in good fighting trim.

Officials in Buffalo sent a telegram to the governor informing him that an illegal posse had invaded Johnson County, killed two citizens, and was resisting arrest by the sheriff. The governor had been in cahoots with the vigilantes all along, so the only news the telegram brought him was the alarming information that his friends were being beaten. He rushed a request off to Washington for troops to lift the siege and save his friends.

Just as the Johnson County men were rolling a clumsy, homemade fortress on wheels toward the fortified house, the cavalry came galloping into view, bugles blaring. The commander accepted the surrender of the besieged gunmen. The sheriff was disgruntled to see the prisoners slip out of his grasp and predicted, correctly as it turned out, that the murderers would get away scot-free. The only one who paid any price for the misadventure was the gunman who had picked off Nick Ray. When he returned to Texas his girl friend fussed at him for his part in the affair. Annoyed by her nagging, he killed her. He was hanged.

In defense of the Johnson County invasion, John Clay, on his return from Europe, wrote, *Great reforms are brought about by revolutionary methods. The Boston tea parties, the victories of Washington were protests flung worldwide against a Teutonic dictator.*

A very curious statement. If there was any dictator involved in the affair, he was not Teutonic but Scottish and named John Clay. If there was any George Washington, it was the sheriff of Johnson County. The only reform brought about was a decline in the despotic power of the Association.

The Cowboy Gone Wrong

WRITERS OF WESTERN books, movies, and television series love to dwell on the shootout between the good guy and the bad guy, a ritual as stereotyped in its steps as a ballet. The bad guy challenges the good guy. They confront each other at opposite ends of the town's main street, glare defiance, and begin a stiff-legged approach while the townfolk scatter. From twenty paces the bad guy reaches for his six-shooter. Like a rattlesnake striking, faster than the eye can follow, the good guy whips out his Colt .45 and drops the bad guy with a single shot that miraculously sheds not a drop of gore.

It didn't happen that way. The working cowboy on the trail usually carried his pistol in his blanket roll, if he carried one at all. Many let it be widely known they were always unarmed in order to avoid fights. Among them were Shanghai Pierce, the great Scottish cattleman Murdo Mackenzie, and the New Mexican cattle baron John Chisum. Many ranchers forbade their cowhands to carry weapons.

There was indeed gunplay in the early days of the far West, but it was rarely between working cowboys. Of the twenty-five men killed in Dodge City, Kansas, in 1872, only one was a cowboy. The rest were gamblers, gangsters, and other riffraff who followed the frontier to take hard-earned money away from cowboys. They were more likely to use

41

The Roundup
by Charles M. Russell

a double-barrelled shotgun or a rifle than a six-shooter, and would consider it stupid to give an intended victim an even break.

Somewhere between the frontier desperado and the hard-working cowboy was a class of gunmen who often slid back and forth across the line separating the law from crime. Men like Bass Outlaw (apparently that was his real name) worked for a while as a Texas Ranger, then reappeared on the scene as a dangerous outlaw. Probably the most dangerous of the breed was a handsome, six foot, two inch young man named Tom Horn.

He ran away from his home in Missouri while he was still a boy. His first job was as a track layer for the Sante Fe Railroad in Kansas. He worked as a cattle-trail driver, drove a stagecoach, mined silver, and wrangled horses for the U. S. Army Cavalry in Arizona.

Eventually, he turned up on the San Carlos Indian Reservation, living with the Apaches, learning their language and their desert lore. He also picked up Spanish from the border Mexicans. Because of these skills, the army hired him as a scout.

Horn led troopers in several running fights with Geronimo, the great Apache chieftain, and was decorated for carrying a wounded sergeant to safety through a rain of gunfire, getting hit in the process. The famous chief of scouts, Al Sieber, suffered a shattered leg in the same fight and Horn took over his job.

Horn interpreted at all the parleys with Geronimo and was the intermediary at his final surrender, thus doing himself out of a job, for there was no further use for scouts once the last Apache warrior was locked up. Horn went to work as a cowboy for the Chiricahua Cattle Company.

Off to town for a little fun between working sessions, Horn entered a dance hall and leaned his rifle against the wall. He wore a six-shooter, but mostly as an ornament, for he depended on his .30-30 carbine for his main armament.

An armed Mexican quarreled with Horn about a dance-hall girl. The Mexican unwisely slapped Horn who knocked him kicking with a single punch. The Mexican drew his revolver and hit Horn once as he plunged across the room for his rifle. Rolling across the floor, Horn pumped the carbine's lever, putting six bullets into the Mexican before he could hit the ground, all of them along the line of his belt.

The fight and killing convinced Horn that working cattle was too tame for somebody of his disposition. He accepted a star as a deputy sheriff.

Once when he was riding after two outlaws, he caught them sleeping in the brush. Though he had them covered with his rifle, when he awakened them they went for their guns. Horn killed one outlaw, but the other shot him in the shoulder. The two men hid in the brush and tried to outwait each other in a daylong stand-off. The outlaw lost patience first. Apparently believing that Horn had died of his wound, the outlaw stepped out of the brush. Horn blew his head off. Authorities had to take Horn's word that he had been forced to shoot the outlaws, but already some westerners were muttering that Horn would rather kill suspects than bring them in for trial.

A crack rodeo hand, Horn was absent at a rodeo, setting a world record for roping, when his boss, the sheriff, was killed by a notorious Indian desperado named the Apache Kid. Feeling that they needed a businesslike lawman more than they did a rodeo champion, county authorities let Horn go. He drifted from job to job as a lawman, but officials began to shy away from hiring him, for he rarely brought in a prisoner, only bodies.

Like many other gunmen, Horn found a job as a range detective, a job that in the wrong hands became a license for killing. As a bounty hunter, a range detective could collect up to $500 for every so-called rustler killed.

Using tracking skills learned from the San Carlos Apaches, he and another detective trailed two train robbers for forty-three days across four states. When they trapped the bandits, the presence of the other detective forced Horn to make them prisoners. Something bad happened at that confrontation, for the other detective refused to work with Horn any further.

After four years of detective work, Horn went to Wyoming to become a range detective for the big ranchers who were trying to scare off small homesteaders they accused of rustling cattle.

Somebody shot down an English homesteader named William Lewis with three closely spaced .30-30 bullets. As part of his campaign to spread fear, Horn bragged openly that he was the killer. When one-armed Fred Powell was shot down on his homestead, some accused Horn of being unsportsmanlike for killing his man from ambush. Horn scoffed.

OVERLEAF:
The Herd Quitter
by Charles M. Russell
COURTESY MONTANA HISTORICAL SOCIETY

"There's no sporting way of killing a man," he said.

To make his position doubly clear, he announced, "Killing men is my specialty. I look at it as a business proposition, and I think I have a corner on the market."

For three years he rode about Wyoming with his .30-30 in a saddle scabbard and a pair of binoculars slung from his saddle horn. To inspire fear, he claimed every unsolved killing in the state. If his claims were true, he killed dozens, which is hardly likely. Later legends hold that he put two rocks under the head of his victims to prove he was the killer, but official reports of the time did not mention that fanciful detail.

When the Spanish-American War broke out, the professional killer rushed to enlist. He came down with fever in Cuba, however, and never saw action.

He returned to Wyoming as the honored guest of big ranchers like John Clay and John Coble of the Iron Mountain Ranch Company.

To break up a nest of rustlers in the Browns Hole country, Horn passed himself off as a simple cowhand named Tom Hicks. He hired himself to Matt Rash, the leader of the Browns Hole community of small

48

ranchers, who may indeed have done a bit of rustling on the side. Rash found a note on his doorstep warning him to leave the country or die. He did not leave and he died. Not only did the man die, but the assassin senselessly killed his horse too.

A famed black bronco rider named Isam Dart took over as leader of the Browns Hole ranchers. He defied a note warning him to leave and urged his followers to stand up like men to the assassin, whoever he was. Dart was shot from ambush. The surviving ranchers of Browns Hole began to realize who Hicks was when he disappeared, and the notes stopped coming.

Somehow, Horn was badly slashed across the neck in a saloon brawl. He went back to his friend Coble at Iron Mountain to recover.

In the Iron Mountain country a sheep rancher named Kels Nickell and James Miller, a cattleman, carried on a feud so serious that neither man ever ventured out without a rifle. Nickell appears to have been a difficult man, for ten years earlier he had wounded Horn's friend Coble in a quarrel about a fence. To make Nickell even less acceptable to Horn, the convalescent range detective fell in love with a school teacher staying with the family of Nickell's enemy Miller.

On July 18, 1901, somebody hid behind a wall of rocks near a gate three-quarters of a mile from the Nickell house. Whoever it was had great experience in bushwhacking, for he had scouted the scene and knew that Nickell would arrive just at sunrise and would dismount to open the gate.

Things went wrong for the assassin, however, because Nickell sent his fourteen-year-old son on an errand to town. To shut out the morning's unseasonable cold, the boy put on his father's coat and hat.

Apparently mistaking the lad for his father, the assassin killed him with two shots, possibly from a .30-30 rifle.

Two weeks later, somebody firing from ambush hit Nickell—for some reason he was unarmed. Though the shots came from 600 yards away, a tremendous range for accurate shooting, Nickell was hit in the left arm, shattering the bone, and again in the left hip and under the right arm. Four masked men killed seventy-five of the Nickell sheep.

U. S. Marshall Joe Lefors, a lawman who later won fame chasing Butch Cassidy and his gang, appeared on the scene and quietly began to investigate the murder of the Nickell boy. Nickell angrily blamed Miller, but Lefors did not believe it.

49

OVERLEAF:
The Strenuous Life
by Charles M. Russell
THE THOMAS GILCREASE INSTITUTE OF
AMERICAN HISTORY AND ART, TULSA, OKLAHOMA

On September 1, 1901, just three weeks after Nickell was shot and his sheep were killed, Tom Horn and his friends won all the riding and roping events of the Cheyenne Frontier Days rodeo. He returned to Iron Mountain to work cattle during the Iron Mountain roundup and accompanied a shipment of cattle to Denver. There he suffered a broken jaw in a saloon brawl.

Back in Wyoming, Lefors was cultivating a friendship with the wife of a rancher who lived near the Nickell place. He tricked her into telling him she had carried sandwiches to Horn while he was waiting in ambush to shoot Nickell. Stenographers hidden behind a partition took down her confession.

Lefors then worked his way into Horn's confidence. As with the rancher's wife, he tricked Horn into bragging of the murder while hidden stenographers recorded his confession.

At Horn's trial, passions ran high. Big ranchers called him the finest lawman and best friend Wyoming had. John Clay took the stand to tell his high regard for the hired gunman. The small ranchers loathed Horn, however, and even Nickell finally came to believe it was Horn and not Miller who killed his son.

Careful reading of the testimony in the trial shows the case against Horn was very weak in spite of his confession, which he denied having made. After all, even if he had bragged to Lefors, he had long had a policy of claiming all murders, including many he could not possibly have committed. Reliable witnesses told of seeing him several days ride away from the ambush site at the time of the killing. Doctors said they thought the bullet holes in the boy were too large to have come from a .30-30, Horn's favorite weapon. The big ranchers contributed huge sums for Horn's defense.

No matter. Horn was found guilty—possibly on the grounds that if he was not guilty of the Nickell murder, he was guilty of enough others to make hanging him worthwhile.

As he awaited execution, Horn coolly watched construction of a gallows in the corridor in front of his cell. Fearing that his friends might try to free him, officials called out two companies of the Wyoming National Guard. Ten deputies posted themselves about the jail building, training rifles on the jail yard.

Horn did overpower a jailer, seize his pistol, and break out of the jail. The weapon he stole was a newfangled automatic Luger, however, and the famed gunman had never seen one before. He had never heard about the safety catch on automatic pistols, and so he struggled without success to get off a shot from the safety-locked pistol. Had he managed to steal a .30-30 carbine he might have escaped.

On his last night on earth, Horn climbed into bed for a nap. The sheriff asked him how he felt.

"Fine," Horn answered. "Why?"

John Coble called on him the next morning for a last goodbye. Coble wept, but Horn did not. He smoked a last cigar and marched firmly to the gallows. He was chatting with witnesses when the trap dropped and he plunged to his death at the end of the hangman's rope.

Anybody can still start a brisk argument in Wyoming on the subject of Horn's guilt or innocence.

Rustling in Wyoming was no better or worse after the departure of the man whose business was killing men, giving the control of cattle thieving as an excuse.

The Cowboy as Lawman

THE WEST HAD many famous lawmen—Wyatt Earp, Bat Masterson, Wild Bill Hickok, Joe Lefors, and dozens of others—but few were working cowboys. Some worked both sides of the law, but not many had a taste for long hours in the saddle following a bawling herd.

One of the toughest lawmen the West ever saw, however, spent most of his youth trailing cattle. He was John Slaughter and looked more like a boy playing sheriff than a dangerous lawman, for he was a little fat man with a baby face, despite a mustache and Vandyke beard he wore to make himself look older.

He was born in 1841 on the Lousiana side of the Texas border, to his everlasting chagrin. His father and mother could not read or write but were highly respected, for shortly after moving to Texas his father fought as a Texas Ranger in the Mexican War and later as a Ranger against Indian raiders.

After a drouth ruined his corn crop, the elder Slaughter gave up farming and turned to cattle ranching. The Slaughters were among the first Texans to import shorthorn bulls for improving the longhorn breed.

In the early 1870s John Slaughter joined half of Texas in rounding up unbranded mavericks and driving them to Kansas. While he was gone on business, his wife and a single black servant, armed with shotguns, held off a band of Comanches through a long night.

A Mexican cheated Slaughter's partner in a cattle deal and Slaughter trailed him across several northern Mexican states to shoot him down. Slaughter was suspected of other gun scrapes, and a posse of vigilantes from San Antonio called at his house. They possibly had the idea of hanging him without trial, for they had long since gone far beyond any reasonable enforcement of order and were hanging right and left on mere whim. It was a good thing for everybody all around that Slaughter was not home, for his later history proves he would not have submitted quietly to hanging.

By the late 1870s, Slaughter felt that Texas was too crowded. Besides, he suffered from asthma and tuberculosis, so he drove a herd across New Mexico headed for Arizona, a territory with a climate reputed good for weak chests.

A band of notorious rustlers headed by a Barney Gallagher rode up to one of Slaughter's trail hands. Gallagher had some kind of grudge against Slaughter, possibly growing out of a card game in San Antonio. He ordered the cowboy to carry a challenge to his boss.

"Tell that little rathead up front I'm here to kill him."

He propped a sawed-off shotgun across his saddle and waited for Slaughter to come into range. He waited longer than he might have, for he could see that Slaughter was not wearing a pistol, and so Gallagher let him trot close enough for a sure kill with the short-range shotgun.

But Slaughter always carried a shotgun, a rifle, and a six-shooter in holsters on his saddle. He whipped out the six-shooter and drilled Gallagher through the heart. The rustler band fled.

Governor Lew Wallace of New Mexico, who was then busy writing the famous novel *Ben Hur*, took time out from his scribbling to order Slaughter arrested for murder. Perhaps somebody pointed out to the governor that Slaughter was in New Mexico on a peaceable errand, driving his cattle, and Gallagher had no good excuse for being on the same ground issuing threats and challenges. Besides, a sawed-off shotgun is hardly a tool of peaceful commerce. So the governor dropped the murder charge but arrested Slaughter anyhow on the grounds that his trail herd included many cattle with strange brands. It is entirely possible that Slaughter, like many other trail bosses, was careless about sweeping up strange cattle along the way, for even his brother-in-law accused him of stealing several hundred head of cattle. The governor felt so strongly

about Slaughter that on his list of wanted criminals Slaughter's name was first and Billy the Kid was fourteenth.

Among the detectives who inspected Slaughter's herd after he was arrested was Charley Siringo. Somehow during the inspection, 500 cattle disappeared. Newspapers openly accused the authorities, including the governor, of arresting Slaughter only so they could steal his cattle.

Siringo followed Slaughter to Arizona, but gave up the plan of going over his herd looking for Texas brands when he discovered the little man, tough enough all by himself, had hired a pack of very mean hombres as his work force.

Slaughter bought a 65,000-acre ranch, partly in Arizona but mostly in Mexico. To stock it, he rode into Mexico on a cattle-buying trip. A Mexican cattle seller pointed out to Slaughter that a band of heavily-armed vaqueros was ready to jump him if he did not dump the silver money from his pack mule. Slaughter whipped out his shotgun, held it to the *hidalgo*'s head and rode to safety with the nervous Mexican as a hostage.

Slaughter's ranch lay on the route Geronimo and his warriors took to Mexico, so his ranch buildings had loopholes for rifles and shotguns. He and his cowboys fought battles with the Indians to recover stolen horses. While he was a scout, Tom Horn operated part of the time from Slaughter's house. Geronimo surrendered on the Slaughter place.

Nearby Tombstone came into existence as a town in 1879, after the discovery of silver. From the beginning, lawmen in the town did not like cowboys. Wyatt Earp, his brothers, and their henchman Doc Holliday brought the town worldwide notoriety as a nest of frontier violence with their famous shootout with cowboys at the OK Corral. After the Earps and Holliday drifted on to other towns, John Slaughter was elected the third sheriff of Cochise County in 1887.

On June 7, 1888, he set the pattern for his administration by killing three Mexican rustlers at dawn with a breech-loading shotgun. A grim western joke had it that the tender-hearted Slaughter tried to kill outlaws in their sleep to spare their feelings.

He kept the jail crowded, but it would have been jammed had he not so often ridden back to town from a manhunt with a body across his saddle or merely with the fugitive's personal gear and weapons. It was a common report that John Slaughter, on the trail of horse thieves, always brought back the horses, but rarely the thieves.

Learning that a notorious thief named Eduardo Moreno was camped on the west side of the Huachuca Mountains, the sheriff took his deputy Burt Alvord across the ridge and jumped the three-man gang. The lawmen killed all the bandits. As usual, Slaughter never explained why the killing was necessary. Alvord later confessed he himself kept $500 he had found on the leader's body. (Alvord later went bad and was suspected of robbing a train while he was town constable.)

Slaughter captured five bank robbers at Willcox. The chief broke loose and fled on horseback, but Slaughter rode him down and returned him to his gang.

Entering a saloon, Slaughter was surprised by a gunman who whipped out his pistol. Darting out his hand, Slaughter got his thumb under the falling hammer, pulled his own weapon and subdued the would-be murderer.

Hoping to lure Slaughter into a trap, train robbers sent a false message that his nephew had been killed at Willcox. Smelling treachery, Slaughter looked up his nephew, found him alive, and boarded the stagecoach for Willcox with a deputy, the two of them loaded for bear. When the stagecoach stopped, they leaped out on opposite sides with cocked shotguns ready for battle. The robbers fled.

Over many years, Slaughter fought a long duel of wits and courage with a famed Mexican outlaw called Augustín Chacón. The Mexican strutted about Tombstone bragging that he would kill Slaughter on sight. The sheriff gave his deputy Alvord a shotgun and crept up on the tent where an informant had told him Chacón was sleeping. Posting Alvord at the front entrance, Slaughter called on Chacón to come out. As Slaughter expected, he plunged out the rear. The sheriff fired, but the bandit tripped on a guy rope, and the charge went over his head. He escaped into Mexico while Slaughter cursed one of his few failures with a shotgun.

On Christmas Eve of 1895, the Chacón gang held up a general store. The manager foolishly refused to open the safe and was duly killed. The sheriff's posse traced the bandits to Morenci where they were holed up in an adobe house, which makes a fine fortress. In the first exchange of fire, two bandits were killed. A Mexican named Pablo Salcido tried to be a peacemaker and was wantonly shot down by Chacón. During the following fracas, Chacón escaped, but was tracked down and jailed. Just ten days before he was to hang, he escaped again and wandered northern Mexico for five years.

(The end of the Chacón adventure came only after Slaughter gave up the sheriff's badge. Alvord tried his hand at banditry. With another ex-lawman named Billy Stiles, he went to Mexico and joined Chacón. Alvord betrayed his boss to Captain Burton C. Mossman, founder of the Arizona Rangers, who arrested Chacón on the Mexican side of the border, brought him back to Arizona, and saw him hanged in 1902.)

Another grudge match with a Mexican bandit began when Sheriff Slaughter sent Deputy Cesario Lucero after Geronimo Baltierrez, who had held up a Wells Fargo pack train of gold. Baltierrez surprised Lucero while the deputy was bent over a spring washing his face. He killed the lawman and fled. Slaughter traced him to Fairbank where he was sleeping in a tent, like Chacón at the previous encounter. The sheriff posted a deputy at each end of the tent and stood to one side, determined not to miss his man the second time. When ordered to come out, Baltierrez cut a slit in the side of the tent and sprinted for the shelter of a fence. Slaughter cut him in two with the shotgun. One of the deputies, new to the job, was so sickened he turned in his badge on the spot. (The same man, incidentally, was later accused of overcoming his sensitivity so successfully that he shot his employer and fled to Oklahoma.)

Slaughter worked out a deal with the famed Col. Emilio Kosterlitzky, colonel of the Mexican *Rurales,* to exchange prisoners across the border, so that thieves could not use the international frontier as a shield.

Retirement as sheriff in 1898 did not end Slaughter's career as a lawman. He became a deputy U. S. Marshal.

Spotting a peg-legged stranger crossing his property at a distance from the ranch headquarters, Slaughter became suspicious of any traveler who avoided his wife's famed hospitality and good cooking. He used the newfangled instrument called a telephone to check with the customs house at Bisbee, Arizona. They told him the stranger was probably Pegleg Finney, wanted for horse stealing.

The exhausted Finney had stretched out to sleep in the shade of a tree with a six-shooter in his hand hidden under his right side. With two assistants, Slaughter stole up on the sleeping man, kicked away his rifle, and ordered him to his feet. Finney swung up the hidden revolver and Slaughter put a huge .45-85 rifle bullet through his gun hand and into his chest. The other two also fired. Any of the three shots would have been enough to kill the horse thief.

Chasing an Indian desperado named the Apache Kid (the desperado who had killed Tom Horn's boss while he was at the rodeo), Slaughter and another tracker took up his trail into the Sierra Madre. At dawn, the two built a brush fire to attract attention, then crept 200 yards away to wait. They saw the Apache Kid sneak up on the fire, hoping to take his pursuers by surprise.

In the bad light of dawn, Slaughter's first shot only wounded the fugitive. The trio began a daylong game of cat and mouse, creeping about and exchanging shots till a long period of silence persuaded Slaughter that the Indian was dead. They found his body pierced by four bullets.

As often happened in the old West, the legend sprang up that it was not really the Apache Kid who had died. For years afterward the Apache Kid was killed in a half-dozen different scrapes by a half-dozen different lawmen or posses.

One gambler who held up a roulette game in Tombstone virtually committed suicide by riding up to Slaughter's front door. Nobody ever understood the purpose of such a stupid maneuver unless he just wanted to get the whole thing over quickly.

Slaughter killed his last man as part of a posse chasing an eighteen-year-old boy who had killed a mother and her son and daughter in a robbery.

Bad health finally forced him to slow down, though he remained a deputy sheriff, mostly an honorary title, till his death in 1922 at the age of eighty-one.

The Cowboy as Artist

THE MAN WHO was to become the most famous of all western artists was born in 1861 in Canton, New York, far from cowboy country. Shortly after his birth, however, his father left the newspaper he edited and joined the Union cavalry; so the youngster grew up around horses and began to draw them from the time he could wrap his fingers around a pencil and push it where he wanted it to go. Like most artists-to-be, Fred Remington was obsessed with drawing and made almost endless sketches of his world in his notebooks, on the margins of books, around the edges of his school papers. And almost always a horse figured somewhere in the drawing—usually a horse going at full gallop, for the boy liked plenty of action in his art.

From the earliest drawings, he showed galloping horses with all four feet off the ground, a practice that won him the ridicule of critics who insisted that a horse always had at least one foot on the ground. It was not till high-speed photography froze galloping horses in midstep that the world discovered the young boy had seen truer than the most experienced horsemen of his day, for the horse can indeed be caught with all four feet off the ground.

To his mother's dismay, Fred was a terrible student. What time he stole from his eternal sketching he spent not at study, but at sports, es-

OVERLEAF:
Turn Him Loose, Bill
by Frederic Remington
COURTESY OF KENNEDY GALLERIES, INC., NEW YORK

pecially riding. His father enjoyed the boy's art and encouraged him, but his mother wanted him to become a good student and later a respectable citizen, preferably a businessman. She wanted him to have no connections in the artistic world which she considered akin to the rootless world of the gypsies.

Somehow, bad a student as he was, he was accepted at Yale and was one of only two students in the newly founded art school. The other student was Poultney Bigelow, who, years later as the editor of the then-important magazine *Outing*, was delighted to discover on his desk some pictures that were, in his words, "the real thing, the unspoiled native genius dealing with Mexican ponies, cowboys, cactus, lariats, and sombreros." It was only after he read the signature that he discovered he had studied with the artist at Yale and had failed, at the time, to recognize his genius. It was Bigelow who gave Remington his first break as a commercial artist.

Remington's father died when the artist was eighteen, leaving him a small sum of money. He went to Montana in 1881. The next year *Harper's Weekly* published a picture of "Cowboys of Arizona: Roused by a Scout." They had thought so little of the original sketch that they had an artist redo it and it was signed, "Drawn by W. A. Rogers from a sketch by Frederic Remington."

Hearing that a Yale schoolmate was sheep ranching in the West, in 1883 Fred used some of his inheritance to buy 160 acres near his friend, just outside of Peabody, Kansas. Being Frederic Remington, he first bought horses; only after being well-mounted on a mare named Terra Cotta did he buy several hundred sheep.

He wrote home that same year a letter with the startling phrase, "—man just shot down the street—must go."

The newspapers of the time record no such shooting. For the rest of his life, Remington indulged a lively imagination that pictured his life as more eventful than it probably was. His art itself rarely shows a tranquil scene, but almost always pictures some violent act happening in a romantic setting. Though the details of his western art were strikingly accurate, the adventures they portrayed were usually imaginary.

He had a lively time as a sheep rancher, losing his horse on a bet, being arrested for acting too frisky at a Christmas Eve party, becoming the local boxing champion, and staying as far away from his flock of sheep as he could manage, for he hated dipping and shearing the animals. He sold the ranch, went back to Canton where he married his boyhood girl friend, and brought her back to the West. She did not like the rough life on the frontier and went home within a year, leaving him behind.

He wandered Arizona and recorded in desperate haste the life of the Apaches, the western soldiery, cowboys—all the pageant and color of the frontier West that was disappearing rapidly before his eyes.

In 1885, Fred took a bundle of his work to New York and called on magazine editors. He made a sale to *Harper's Weekly*, this time enjoying a credit line all to himself. He sold to his old schoolmate Bigelow at *Outing*. He began selling regularly to the best-paying magazines of the day. In 1888 he illustrated Theodore Roosevelt's *Ranch Life and the Hunting Trail*, the president-to-be's account of his years as a rancher in the Dakota Badlands.

Satisfied that he was going to spend at least part of his time in the East, his wife rejoined him. For the rest of his life, Remington spent at least three months of every year in the West, polishing his style and making sketches for the coming nine months of work in New York.

He went on grizzly bear hunts, though his tendency to gain weight forced him to choose big powerful horses rather than the agile ponies he would have preferred for the mountain trails of the New Mexican bear country.

Remington also turned to writing. In *Pony Tracks* he reported on his adventures during his western visits.

On a hunt in the Mexican state of Chihuahua, he says a Mexican companion rode thirty-six hours without rest and broke down two horses to bring the party a new supply of pipe tobacco. He also writes casually about two women being shot in a nearby house in a hail of lead. Remembering Remington's vivid imagination, some historians raise their eyebrows about the violence that seemed to follow him everywhere. There is no evidence the shootings really happened—or didn't happen, for that matter.

He certainly did join a cavalry patrol across Yellowstone Park in its first days as a national wildlife reserve. Worried about the geysers squirting hot water and steam all about him, Remington wrote, *They rode recklessly over the geyser formations to my discomfort, because it is very thin and hazardous and to break through is to be boiled. One instinctively objects to that form of cooking.*

He noted that winter patrols crossed the snows on a newfangled contraption he called "the *ski* or Norwegian snowshoe."

The patrol deliberately left its tracks across the wilderness areas of the park as a warning to illegal fur trappers and hunters that law enforcers were on the prowl. Remington was enthusiastic about the park.

It is a great game preserve and breeding ground, and, if not disturbed, must always give an overflow [of game] into Montana, Wyoming, and Idaho, which will make big game shooting there for years to come. The ... disregard of the American pioneer for game laws and game preservation is somewhat excusable, but the lines of the pioneer are now cast in new places, and his days of lawless abandon *are done. The regulation for the punishment of Park offenders is inadequate and should be made more severe.*

Any park visitor so coarse as to write his name on "her sacred face" deserved nothing short of six months in jail, according to Remington.

In 1890, Remington, in his rush to record the last days of the frontier West, joined the U. S. Army cavalry in their campaign against the warring Sioux Indians in the Dakotas, the same campaign that included the extermination of General Custer's command. Despite the load of fat he took into the field, he kept up with the tough cavalrymen, riding sixty miles in one day on a single horse, an animal that must have been a powerful brute to carry 240 pounds over that grinding route.

Remington and his troop had several encounters with hostile Sioux and the artist carried a rifle throughout the campaign. He missed the last Indian battle of the West, but later rode to the camp of the Seventh United States Cavalry to talk with the survivors of that Battle of Wounded Knee.

The Sioux warriors had been told that they wore magic shirts that would turn aside the white man's bullet. A cavalry officer told Remington how the battle started.

. . . the trouble began when the old medicine man threw the dust in the air. That is the old Indian sign of "defiance," and no sooner had he done that act than those bucks stripped and went into action. Just before that someone told me that if we didn't stop that old man's talk he would make trouble. He said that the white men's bullets would not go through the ghost shirts.

Another officer remarked with admiration on the professional skill of the Indian riflemen.

One man was hit early in the firing, but he continued to pump his Winchester; but growing weaker and weaker, and sinking down gradually, his shots went higher and higher, until his last went straight up in the air.

A soldier told Remington that the dying braves were bitter about the lies told them by their medicine man.

One young warrior who was near to his death asked me to take him over to the medicine man's side, that he might die with his knife in the old conjurer's heart. He had seen that the medicine was bad, and his faith in the ghost shirt had vanished.

Three days later, on the train going back East, Remington read of the death of the young officer who had been his comrade during the campaign.

Finally, there was no doubt; Remington had indeed been around some serious shooting and nobody could charge the scenes of that last Indian fight to his imagination.

After gaining great fame in the East, Remington died in Ridgefield, Connecticut, in 1909 at the age of forty-eight.

The Black Cowboy

BOOKS, MOVIES, AND television shows almost always show the cowboy as a white man of distinctly Anglo-Saxon or Celtic features—clearly the son of English or Scottish parents. Yet records show that at least one-third of the working cowboys on the great trail drives were Mexican, more rarely pure Indian, and freedmen of Afro-American black ancestry. The half-Indian Mexican vaquero had long been the pattern for the cowboy in Texas. Few historians record, however, how many hundreds or even thousands of slaves, freed during the Civil War, took to the cowboy's life and made good at it.

Though some black cowboys like Bill Pickett, the rodeo star who invented the art of bulldogging, made a bigger name, none ranks higher in history than George McJunkin, the freedman from Texas who ran two huge ranches in New Mexico and discovered the site of what a distinguished archaeologist flatly calls "the most important discovery in the field of North American prehistory."

Stories of his birth and youth are confused and contradictory.

He was certainly born about 1856 in south Texas. Some stories say he was born free, but it hardly seems likely, for virtually all blacks in south Texas at that date were slaves. Probably his owner was named McJunkin, for it was a custom for black freedmen and women who had no last names as slaves to take the name of their former owner.

Before he left home some time in his mid-teens, he had learned to speak Spanish from the vaqueros on his ranch, and they had also taught him to be a crack rider and roper. He left home on a mule—whether stolen or borrowed is not clear, and perhaps the young lad was not clear on that fine moral point either, for all kinds of stock roamed the range free for the taking right after the Civil War. He did explain in later years that he chose a mule rather than a horse because a black riding the humbler animal would cause less comment.

At Comanche, a savagely antiblack town at the time, he bought his first pair of cowboy boots—indeed his first foot gear of any kind—with money made by digging a well.

Suitably shod and thus able to pass for a cowhand, he got a job with a trail herd as a wrangler, a low-caste job that required caring for the spare horses and helping the cook. At the end of the trail in Dodge City, Kansas, he found that a black youth was not welcome in the usual cowboy haunts, so he drifted back to the chuck wagon, the only home he had. He did bring with him a proper cowboy hat, a saddle, and his own horse, bought with his wrangler wages.

He spent the winter of 1868 at his father's home in Texas, but in spring rode back to Comanche for a promised second trail job. Along the way, he fell in with a large herd of horses being driven west by Gideon Roberds, his brother, Mrs. Roberds, and an adopted son, Jabe Burton. A horse broke away from the herd and McJunkin rode it down, neatly lassoing it on the run. Impressed by his horsemanship, Gideon offered him a job as a breaker of wild horses.

McJunkin was in a pinch. To go from being a slave to a man choosing between two jobs was a jolt. He joined the Roberds family.

They first pastured their herd in the Palo Duro Canyon that slashes across the dry High Plains of the Texas Panhandle. (One of the last herds of longhorns in the world still grazes in Palo Duro Canyon.) Comanches ran off the horses. Apparently the Roberds brother was killed by the Indians.

McJunkin seems to have left the Roberds family for a time, working cattle on the Dry Cimarron River at the spot where New Mexico, Oklahoma, Texas, and Colorado are almost within sight of each other. He rejoined the Roberds family in a horse-breaking venture on the Picketwire River in Colorado. (The Picketwire gets its curious name from the

English-speaking cowboys' mispronunciation of the French name that means the Purgatory River.) Horses trained by McJunkin for cutting calves out of a herd without signals from the rider became sought after in the high country.

As the years passed, he taught the Roberds boys to ride and rope; they taught him to read and write. Some say he had a fourth-grade education before leaving Texas, but it is doubtful, for owners did not waste education on slaves. Besides, a fourth-grade education offered a black boy in that day and place would not have amounted to much.

McJunkin was a natural student and became an avid reader of any printed matter he could get his hands on. He spent his spare time in the little Mexican-Spanish towns learning to play the guitar and violin.

He was sent to a branch of the gigantic 101 Ranch in Oklahoma as a helping hand for a roundup. Dr. Thomas E. Owen, one of the ranch partners, hired him to handle a herd of thoroughbred race horses on a new ranch back in the Dry Cimarron Valley McJunkin had known as a cowboy. Although Dr. Owen had been a Confederate Army officer, McJunkin sat at the table with the doctor's family. At the last roundup before barbed wire closed off the open range forever, McJunkin was wagon boss for two ranches, putting him in charge of 200 horses and thousands of cattle, plus a hundred white cowboys.

McJunkin received as a gift a surveyor's transit, the sighting telescope used to lay off exact boundary lines, and he supervised stringing of the first fences. Because of his skill with the surveyor's tools, he settled many boundary arguments on the High Plains.

During a terrible blizzard in 1889, McJunkin and his cowboys were caught in the open working a large herd of cattle. They feared they might freeze, but McJunkin led them to the cabin of Harvy Bramblett who had left a lamp burning in the window according to the High Plains custom during a snowstorm.

The storm held them snowbound for ten days and almost wiped out Owen's herd. But the cowboys survived.

Dr. Owen suffered severe losses in the storm and died two years later. McJunkin went to work for William H. Jack at a neighboring ranch. Mrs. Jack noticed the black cowboy's eager interest in books, so she made him a present of an encyclopedia and books on astronomy and other sciences. He devoured them all, committing great stretches to memory.

A high-powered army telescope was McJunkin's next acquisition. According to one story, a retired army engineer gave it to him because of his interest in the stars. Another story has it that he rescued an army paymaster being beaten by four bandits in the desert. After driving off the robbers, the cowboy asked the lieutenant about the strange tube he was carrying in a rifle scabbard. The officer showed him how to use the telescope and gave it to him out of gratitude for the rescue. McJunkin had a saddlemaker fashion a scabbard for the telescope and never again rode without it. He used it to spot brands on distant cattle during the day and to study the heavens at night.

In 1908, a terrible flood devastated the nearby town of Folsom. Riding the range to see what damage had been done, McJunkin noted that the raging waters had sliced a deep new cutbank on Wild Horse Arroyo. McJunkin knew the spot well, for he had dug fossils and bones there and added them to his collection of curios. The flood had laid bare, however, bones such as he had never seen before—great knobby joints and leg bones for animals twice the size of the biggest steer on the ranch.

McJunkin always wore a white shirt and clean clothes to show that a good cowhand did not have to get dirty if he knew his job. He was so excited by the big bones, however, that he slid into the pit, splashing mud on his neat costume in his eagerness to dig out some specimens for his collection. He carried them home, looked up what he could find

about such huge creatures, and passed the word to anybody who would listen about his great find. Few paid much attention, for a deep interest in archeology in that ranch country belonged almost entirely to the lone black cowboy.

But not quite entirely. A young friend expressed interest and together in the winter of 1918 they visited the site. They dug out some bones and a spear point and took them to a local amateur archeologist. Excited by the find and suspecting that it was a big one, the amateur carried the finds to the Colorado Museum of Natural History in Denver.

Unaccountably, museum experts showed little interest.

At sixty-five years of age, McJunkin fell ill. His house burned with his precious collections. He moved to town and on January 21, 1922, he died, his tremendous find at Wild Horse Arroyo still unknown to science.

Four years later Dr. J. D. Figgins of the Denver Museum brought a crew to Wild Horse Arroyo to find out what, after all, the black cowboy had discovered in that cutbank.

At that time, all scientists agreed that Indians had come from Asia to the New World only about 3,000 years ago.

Almost immediately after Dr. Figgins and his crew began to dig, they found the bones of animals that had disappeared from North America 10,000 years ago. They found one spear point made by man, but it was not definitely linked to the bones and just might have been carried in by the flood.

When they found a spearpoint jammed into the bones of a giant buffalo that had been extinct for 10,000 years, however, there was no longer any doubt. A man smart enough to make beautiful stone spearpoints had lived in North America and hunted creatures that died out 10,000 years ago.

Since that find, called the Folsom Site after the nearby town of Folsom, New Mexico, scientists have uncovered many other sites pushing man's presence in North America farther and farther back in time. (It is curious that a startlingly high percentage of those sites were found by amateurs like McJunkin.)

No find before or since has shaken up the scientists concerned with early man in North America like that beautiful little fluted spear head called the Folsom Point, discovered and almost forced on an indifferent world by the greatest of the black cowboys, George McJunkin of New Mexico.

The Cowboy as Showman

Beginning in the last part of the nineteenth century, audiences in the tame East paid large sums of money to be entertained by ropers, riders, marksmen, and Indians from the Wild West. Buffalo Bill and Pawnee Bill and a dozen other celebrities from the frontier organized what they called Wild West shows and traveled the settled areas of the East and even overseas to carry some of the West's glamor to a world that had only read about the frontier and wanted to share its excitement.

The most successful cowboy showman of all was a quarter-breed Cherokee named Will Rogers, who became a kind of homespun philosopher-spokesman for the nation during the 1920s and 1930s.

Will was born on November 4, 1879, near Coffeeville, Kansas, on the lands of the Cherokee Nation in what is now Oklahoma. His father was a prosperous farmer and cattle rancher. Will had his own pony on his fifth birthday; when he was nine he was working as a cowboy at the roundup.

Most important for his career, he became friendly with a black cowboy named Dan Walker who was a wizard with a lariat. Will practiced hours daily under Walker's supervision till, as he put it in later years, he could "lasso a prairie dog."

He went to several schools but was a poor student. At the Scarritt

Collegiate Institute in Neosho, Missouri, the headmaster warned him several times to quit fooling around with a rope and get down to business. When he lassoed the headmaster's colt and the frightened colt and its mother ran off, the headmaster gave Will a ticket home.

In 1893, he went to the Chicago World's Fair. He attended Buffalo Bill's Wild West Show and was entranced by the rope work of Vincente Oropeza of Puebla, Mexico, probably the greatest rope artist who ever lived. The *charro* (as the Mexican gentleman-cowboy is called) could write his name in the air one letter at a time by twirling his lariat in fancy patterns. From that moment, the lariat became Will's obsession.

He reported to Kemper Military School at Boonville, Missouri, dressed in a stage cowboy outfit and carrying in his luggage an assortment of lariats. His school work did not improve, except that he discovered a liking for American history and a skill at public speaking. He could not resist hamming up his most serious recitations to the delight of his fellow students, but to the dismay of serious-minded teachers.

When he turned eighteen, he discovered he had so many demerits it would take 150 hours of marching to work them off. Unable to face a month of eight-hour days of walking, a most distasteful job for a cowboy, he left school and took a job as a horse wrangler and ranch hand in Texas.

Like a typical cowboy, he rambled the West, working cattle in New Mexico and California. He won his first roping prize at Claremore, Oklahoma, in 1899. Increasingly unhappy with the taming of the Wild West, he decided to go to Argentina where he had heard the cattle frontier still existed.

Somehow the ship he took for Argentina wound up in England. Desperately seasick, the young cowboy staggered off the ship and vowed that he would spend the rest of his life as an Englishman unless somebody built a bridge back to the United States.

The human mind forgets the worst ordeals, however, and Will recovered his nerve for the sea voyage to Buenos Aires, where he arrived in May, 1902. Nobody was hiring cowboys in Argentina, so Will soon ran out of money and had to sleep in the park. During the day, he wandered about the city and, led by the cowboy's instinct, found himself at the stockyards where workers were trying to load a shipment of mules. The stubborn animals refused to be caught, however, and the Argentine stockyard men were worn out from the chase. As always,

Will had a lariat in hand, so he flipped out the loop and roped a mule. The astonished manager offered him a coin for every mule he caught. Will settled down to the work he liked best, roping mules right through the lunch hour and filling his pockets.

Because of his reputation as a roper, Will got a job tending cattle on a ship headed for South Africa. In Johannesburg, South Africa, the homesick cowboy discovered a touring company called Texas Jack's Wild West Show. It was a shabby little outfit, but it looked like home to Will who got a job as the "Cherokee Kid, who can lasso the tail off a blowfly." It was his first taste of show business.

Going home the long way, he sailed for New Zealand and did his rope act there with a traveling circus. The locals had never seen rope tricks and his act was a huge success. A newspaper said he could lasso "the business end of a flash of lightning."

After two years of wanderings, Will came home to Claremore, Oklahoma, on a freight train, ending a 50,000 mile trip around the globe. His brief career as an entertainer had changed his life. After a short rest, he went to the St. Louis World's Fair in 1903 and did his rope act in Colonel Zack Mulhall's Wild West Show. He went with the show to New York City for an appearance in Madison Square Garden.

During a performance before a packed house, a longhorn steer leaped from the arena into the stands, scattering frightened customers like a covey of quail. The steer thrashed about looking for an escape and threatened to impale some luckless customer on his rack of horns.

Will's rope snaked out and looped around the brute's neck. Holding the animal steady, Will soothed it and coaxed it back to the ring.

The newspapers made exciting copy out of the Oklahoma Indian who had saved innumerable lives by his cowboy skill in subduing a raging beast. Will probably smiled to himself over the heated prose of the news stories, for he had roped and handled ten thousand longhorns on the range where nobody so much as raised an eyebrow over his skill. But he was a smart enough showman to encourage the publicity.

Because of the publicity about the runaway longhorn, he got a job in the rooftop show at the Victoria Music Hall in New York, the biggest showplace in North America at the time. His biggest problem was getting his horse into the elevator before and after every show. His roommate during this period, incidentally, was a young cowboy who later became the nation's top western movie star as Tom Mix.

Constantly improving his act, Will worked out a three-rope cast, one loop catching the running horse's neck, one the horse's body, and the third the rider. Then he developed a figure eight single-rope throw that flipped one loop over the horse's neck, the other over the rider. His act was a huge success in the United States and later in Paris, Berlin, and London.

He organized a Wild West Show and suffered a bad financial loss. A theater manager asked him why he fooled around with a big herd of horses, a troop of performers, and all the paraphernalia of a traveling circus when the audience wanted to watch only the star roper. He rid himself of the show and returned to solo appearances.

He began cracking jokes while he twirled his rope and discovered his audiences were tickled by his simple cowboy humor, so much so that his patter became more important to his act than his rope. He injured his right arm in a diving accident, so he added more jokes while he did a reduced number of tricks with his left hand.

Will tired of his own hick jokes, so he began to make funny comments about the news of the day. He coined a line that became his trademark.

"Well, all I know is what I read in the newspapers," he would say while he twirled his lariat, and even his fellow performers would gather in the wings to hear what was his line of patter for the day.

Will did a show for a club of society ladies; it was a flop. He did the same show for the prisoners at Sing Sing Penitentiary; it was a great success. Will figured it out. The society ladies rarely read the newspapers and had no idea what he was joking about; the prisoners read every line they could get their hands on. Incidentally, before speaking at dinners he stopped at a diner to fill up on cowboy fare of chili con carne and enchiladas to avoid eating the usual canned peas and fried chicken.

In the mid-1920s, he traveled in Europe and sent back articles pretending to be from a diplomat reporting to the president. He started sending daily telegrams of comment on the news to American newspapers and for the rest of his life wrote that daily dispatch no matter where he was or what he was doing—making a movie on a desert location, crossing the Atlantic on a steamer, hobnobbing with the leaders of Europe.

On his return from abroad in 1926, he chatted with Franklin D. Roosevelt, who was later to become one of the most illustrious presidents of American history. That shrewd politician and student of foreign affairs said of the Oklahoma Indian, "Will Rogers' analysis of affairs abroad was not only more interesting but proved to be more accurate than any other I had heard." Will had come a long way from a trick roper in a Wild West show.

For his act, Will joked about his fear of flying. "Here I was thousands of feet up in the air when you can't even get me to ride a tall horse." In fact, he was an early enthusiast for aviation.

"I always told you we have the aviators," he wrote. "Just give them the planes. I have flown in the past year with at least a dozen boys whom I wouldn't be afraid to start to Siberia with."

(That last statement was grimly prophetic, for Will's last flight was en route to Siberia.)

He became obsessed with aviation and complained that European countries were outstripping the United States at the very art two Americans had invented. To fly about the country before the days of airlines, he had to take mail planes, paying postage on himself as though he was a parcel post package.

Because he had sent his daily telegram from Chicago with a Cleveland dateline, he insisted on flying to Cleveland through a terrible blizzard. His pilot on that dangerous trip, incidentally, was one of the first female commercial pilots.

So faithful was Will to his daily telegram that as he was being wheeled into surgery for a gallstone operation, he dictated his dispatch for that day and the following day when he would still be groggy from ether.

Over one of the first nationwide radio network broadcasts, Will imitated the voice of President Calvin Coolidge. He cracked a lot of jokes not suitable to the dignity of a president. He was so good a mimic that half the listeners thought it was the president speaking and expressed horror at his frivolous conduct. Will apologized to the president; Coolidge, a rather glum man, gave a rare smile and told Will he had enjoyed the show.

Will's good show business friend, Fred Stone, was badly hurt just before opening night of his musical *Three Cheers* in which he was to star. Will cancelled all of his own engagements, at great loss, and took his friend's place. He had never rehearsed the part, so he carried the script in his pocket and pulled it out to consult it whenever he forgot a line. The audience was delighted. He soon abandoned the script and improvised a different show every night, commenting about American politics. Sometimes when he got to rolling smoothly, the show lasted an hour or more longer than scheduled. It was his last stage appearance and it was a triumph.

He went to Hollywood, where the invention of talking pictures had made the screen perfectly suited for his wisecracking act. For the rest of his life, he ranked first or, at worst, second, as a box office attraction. In Hollywood style, producers gave their cowboy star an elaborate dressing room with fireplace, couch, private bath, all the fripperies that go with stardom. However, between takes on the set, Rogers could be found, not in his fancy dressing room, but in the backseat of his car banging out his daily articles on a typewriter in his lap.

Through the days of worldwide fame and great riches, Will remained a cowboy. He never walked when he could ride a horse. He had a huge California estate, but spent most of his spare time at a corral roping calves. The only sport he learned was polo, because he could play it from horseback. For the sake of his guests, he put in a few holes of golf on his estate, but he never played. Sometimes he would show up on the golf course, galloping a polo pony and driving golf balls back to the players with a polo mallet.

Even after he had become the philosopher and spokesman for the American common man and the top-ranking movie star of the world, he was still obsessed with the lariat he had first started to twirl for the black cowboy teacher in the Cherokee Nation. He could not sit still through a whole formal dinner, but would jump up and practice roping while continuing his conversation with startled guests. Occasionally, he would playfully rope a dinner partner. Ed Borein, the western artist, got so tired of being roped at Will's house that he bought him a stuffed calf to work with during his dinner practice sessions, thus sparing the guests.

On being invited to go big game hunting in Alaska, Will said he was not a hunter. "I just don't want to be shooting any animal." But he did want to see Alaska. With his friend and fellow Oklahoman, the famed pilot Wiley Post, he planned a trip to Siberia by way of Alaska. Because of all the water along the route, Post installed two heavy pontoon floats on his plane. The outsize rig made the plane dangerously nose-heavy, but Post, an experienced pilot, thought he was good enough to handle the problem.

Will packed two cases of chili con carne into the plane and the pair took off for the north.

They crossed the vast land of Alaska from the south to the Arctic coast. Lost in a storm, Post found a hole in the clouds and set down on a lagoon. Eskimo fishermen told him where he was and how to find Barrow, the farthest northern town in the United States. Post taxied to the end of the lagoon, revved up, and roared across the water, taking off just before hitting the far shore.

The Eskimos watched the plane climb and bank toward Barrow. The motor sputtered and died. Without power, Post could not hold it in the air. The nose-heavy plane, dragged down by its pontoons, plunged like a rock into the lagoon.

The word flashed from the little Eskimo town of Barrow to the outside world: America's beloved cowboy-philosopher was dead.

The *New York Times* gave over four full pages to the news. The Columbia Broadcasting System and National Broadcasting Company observed a half-hour of radio silence in his memory. Movie houses closed. In New York a squadron of planes towing long black mourning streamers flew over the city.

To this day, many visitors to far-off Barrow trudge across the tundra to see the marker of Oklahoma stone that reads, *Will Rogers and Wiley Post ended life's flight here August 15, 1935.*

The Cowboy as Rodeo Star

MANY NON-WESTERNERS CONFUSE rodeo with the Wild West show, assuming that the events are rehearsed and the performers are actors, with the winners determined in advance like a professional wrestling show. Far from it. The contestants put up stiff entry fees and are competing hard for the prize money. Rodeo performers are as tough and well-conditioned a pack of athletes as exist in the world of sports and few can match their ferociously competitive spirit.

Roping and steer-wrestling contests are timed events. Riding of broncs and bulls is judged by style, for all rides are cut off in either eight or ten seconds. Once bronc riders rode the wild horses till they gave up and admitted the man was the boss. But that was when the prairie swarmed with unbroken horses. Now, the bulls and broncs are allowed to feel as though they have beaten the man when he jumps off after the whistle blows. That keeps the animals mean and aggressive.

Those animals are perhaps the most pampered in the world. In a year's competition, they won't be in the arena more than five or, at the most, ten minutes. For those few moments of fury, they live a life of luxury. Some horses like Midnight and Five Minutes to Midnight are more famous than most rodeo champions, so famous they are buried at the Cowboy Hall of Fame.

81

OVERLEAF:
Stampeded by Lightning
by Frederic Remington
THE THOMAS GILCREASE INSTITUTE OF
AMERICAN HISTORY AND ART, TULSA, OKLAHOMA

Western historians solemnly record that the first rodeo was in 1883 at Pecos, Texas, when for the first time contests determined who was the best rider and who the best roper in the West. Or was it three years later in Albuquerque, New Mexico, when a seventy-five dollar saddle given the winner of the riding contest put the show on a serious competitive basis? Or was it in Wyoming about the same time when the Two Bar Cattle Company entertained 150 visiting Scottish and English shareholders with an exhibition of racing, bareback riding, bronc busting, and roping by the ranch's 200 cowboys? (The pistol champion of that show, incidentally, changed his name from Parker to Butch Cassidy when he went into the bank-robbing business.)

The fact is that vaqueros first and cowboys later tested their skills against each other as far back into history as we can trace the western cattle kingdom. Texas history records a contest at San Antonio in 1843 between Texas Rangers, Mexican vaqueros, and Comanche warriors. Judges passed out pistols and bowie knives as prizes. First in riding went to a Florida cowboy, second to a Comanche, and third to a *ranchero* from south of the Rio Grande.

Perhaps the longest continuous rodeo is the Frontier Days, begun in 1897 at Cheyenne, Wyoming.

The first contests were to test ranchworthy skills like breaking wild horses or roping calves. Soon contestants began to invent contests with no earthly use to a cowboy. Bill Pickett, a black Texan cowboy, got bored with the usual riding and roping contests he was winning regularly, so he tried a new stunt. Leaping from a running horse to the neck of a fleeing steer, he twisted the animal's nose skyward by the horns, locked his teeth in the steer's lip, and jerked the half-ton of beef off its feet by the muscles of his jaw and neck. Other cowboys imitated his act, but for lack of Pickett's remarkable teeth and jaws, they threw their steers by twisting their heads till they had to drop or suffer a broken neck. (Pickett was killed not in his dangerous rodeo specialty but by a sorrel horse that kicked him in the head.)

In 1871 in Erath County, Texas, an accidental explosion of Christmas fireworks destroyed an eye and hideously scarred the face of a red-headed thirteen-year-old named Samuel Privett. Because of his scary appearance, he was from that day known as Booger Red and he advertised himself as the world's ugliest man. Whether he honestly owned that championship or not, he did become perhaps the greatest bronc rider who ever lived.

Booger Red went on tour, offering to ride any man's worst outlaw horse—not just ride him, but ride him backwards or with no hands if the owner insisted. He paid his way by passing the hat through the crowd. As organized rodeo grew, his appearances became more regular. He was virtually unbeatable at his specialty of bronc riding and he ruled the rodeo circuit till he retired from old age. He may have retired too soon, for in 1926 at a Fort Worth, Texas, rodeo, the announcer recognized him in the stands and introduced him. The announcer casually mentioned, "it would be something to see Booger Red ride one." The crowd went wild and the show could not go on till the 68-year-old veteran, sick with kidney disease, made one more ride. He died two months later and is still celebrated as the greatest rodeo rider of all time.

Late in the nineteenth century there appeared from Mexico a charro named Vincente Oropeza who was a magician with a lariat. It was Señor Oropeza who inspired Will Rogers to become the world's best-known roper, but it was also Will Rogers who said "No other roper had such accuracy and style as Vincente Oropeza." He introduced the art of fancy roping as a rodeo event.

Other all-time greats are Jim Shoulders, Casey Tibbs, Leonard Stroud, Dean Oliver, Jackson Sundown, the movie actor Yakima Canutt, Pete Knight, Harry Hopkins, and Fritz Truan. Many fans, trying the impossible task of rating the absolutely greatest all-around rodeo cowboy, vote for Gene Rambo. (Was Joe Louis a better boxer than Muhammed Ali? How can anybody attempt to compare athletes who lived in different times?)

The current reigning champion is a good-natured extrovert, highly skilled at public relations and a tiger in the rodeo ring, named Larry Mahan. He won five consecutive all-around cowboy world championships and it looks like he will go on winning them till old age brings him down. Most modern rodeo events have little relation to practical cowboy work, and so rodeo champions are likely to be great athletes rather than practical cowhands. They are also quite likely to be skilled businessmen. Larry Mahan, at least, knows how to parlay his athletic skill and appealing personality into a respectable dollar. He flies his own plane, endorses products for Madison Avenue advertising agencies, and behaves with the canny business sense of any good money manager.

Larry Mahan's chief rival was Phil Lyne, a slight youth who flashed onto the rodeo scene, promptly took two consecutive all-around championships from Mahan, then retired at the age of twenty-seven.

85

Stories circulating around the rodeo world credit the youthful Phil Lyne with performances that would be dismissed as legendary if living witnesses did not exist by the hundreds.

The calf roper, for instance, is almost entirely dependent on his horse. A well-trained horse is 90 percent of the act and the champion calf roper normally has won the event months earlier in long hours of patient work with his horse that pay off in the few seconds they appear together in the arena. Not so with Phil Lyne. He didn't own a roping horse. In one year of his brief career he rode ninety-one horses in roping competition.

Witnesses swear that once he dashed onto the rodeo grounds just as the loudspeaker blared his name for the next calf. He asked a passing cowboy if he could borrow his horse, rode the strange animal to the starting line, and roped his animal in a stunning 10.5 seconds, near a world record.

Among rodeo people themselves, the most respected performer of all time is Bill Linderman, first cowboy to win three national championships in one year (steer wrestling, saddle bronc riding, and all-around cowboy in 1950) and first to win all-around twice in 1950 and 1953.

He was born at Bridger, Montana, in 1920 and in his teens became a hard-rock miner, a gruelling job that gave him powerful arms and shoulders. He left the mines to break wild horses on the Crow Indian Reservation. Passing through Greeley, Colorado, while a rodeo was underway, he happened to register in the saddle bronc contest and took the $300 prize money.

Asked years later why he worked in such a dangerous profession as rodeo, Bill said, "That $300 I won at Greeley for riding a mean horse was twice what I got for riding mean horses for a month at the ranch. That showed me the way. Where else but in rodeo can a dumb cowboy like me with no education earn money like a movie star makes?"

Bill did indeed make big money—almost half a million dollars before the end. But he did it the hard way.

Asked at the Cheyenne Frontier Days how many bones he had broken, Bill replied, "Headbone for one, fractured my skull, that is. Broke my neck and back in the same accident in Deadwood, South Dakota, when a bull fell on me. Broke my right arm four times. Broke a leg twice. Ribs? Lost count. Hands and feet more or less broken. Collarbone. Oh, if you're going to count collarbones. Yeah, I broke my collarbones quite a bit, but I can't remember the exact count."

Rodeo events and performers are roughly divided into two lots: ropers and riders. Ropers perform in the calf-roping and steer-wrestling events, for instance, and riders are competing in the saddle bronco and bareback events. Obviously, a cowboy who must throw a calf weighing 200 pounds or more has to have a bit of muscle and the cowboy who wrestles a half-ton of horned steer to the ground has to have plenty of muscle. The ropers, therefore, are big men, muscular and sometimes even downright fat, like weight lifters. Riders are more like jockeys, slender and quick and beautifully coordinated.

Unlike most steer wrestlers, Bill was not a giant. He stood only six feet tall and never weighed more than 175 pounds, but it was all leather-hard muscle. Possessed of a fiery temper, Bill was respected as the toughest brawler on the circuit.

A story began the rounds of the rodeo circuit that Casey Tibbs, driving Bill to the Cheyenne rodeo, stopped sixty miles out on the range and asked Bill to check a tire. According to the story, for a prank, Casey drove off, leaving Bill to hitchhike into town. Those who knew Bill best say the story couldn't be true because Casey Tibbs is still alive.

Except for his admitted physical strength packed into a compact package, Bill did not have natural rodeo talents like the dazzling timing of Phil Lyne. He was only an average athlete. What he had was a savage will to win that drove him like a demon.

George Williams, the rodeo specialist at the Cowboy Hall of Fame, tells a story typical of Linderman's hard drive. During the uranium prospecting boom, Linderman went into the Arizona wilderness with four other rodeo cowboys to try their luck at finding a fortune. He agreed to stay at the campsite cutting firewood while the others struck out to the four points of the compass. When the prospectors returned at the end of the day, Linderman had a mountainous stack of beautifully split and sized wood, enough firewood to last them through ten hard winters —and was still splitting steadily on, determined that he would set the all-time record for stacking firewood.

Long after rodeo had become big-time show business, drawing large crowds all over the country and pouring money into box offices, the performers themselves were miserably paid, often cheated out of their small prize money, forced to live in ratty little hotels—in general, treated like hangers-on rather than the very heart and soul of the business. Rodeo performers to this day prefer competing for prize money, refusing the idea of accepting salaries or in any other way losing their independence. But they naturally want their share of the box office take to be somewhere near fair. And they don't like being cheated out of their winnings any more than anybody else. So they organized, and the sport today is policed by the Rodeo Cowboys Association, with its headquarters in Denver. Business practices are regulated and rodeo conduct supervised by the association officers, themselves all rodeo performers.

Bill Linderman was one of the founders of the association. He was so highly respected that for six years he was elected president. On November 11, 1965, he was flying to Spokane, Washington, for a meeting about rodeo business. His jet crashed at Salt Lake City, Utah, and he died in the flames.

The King, as he was affectionately known in the cowboy world, had literally given his life for rodeo.

Index

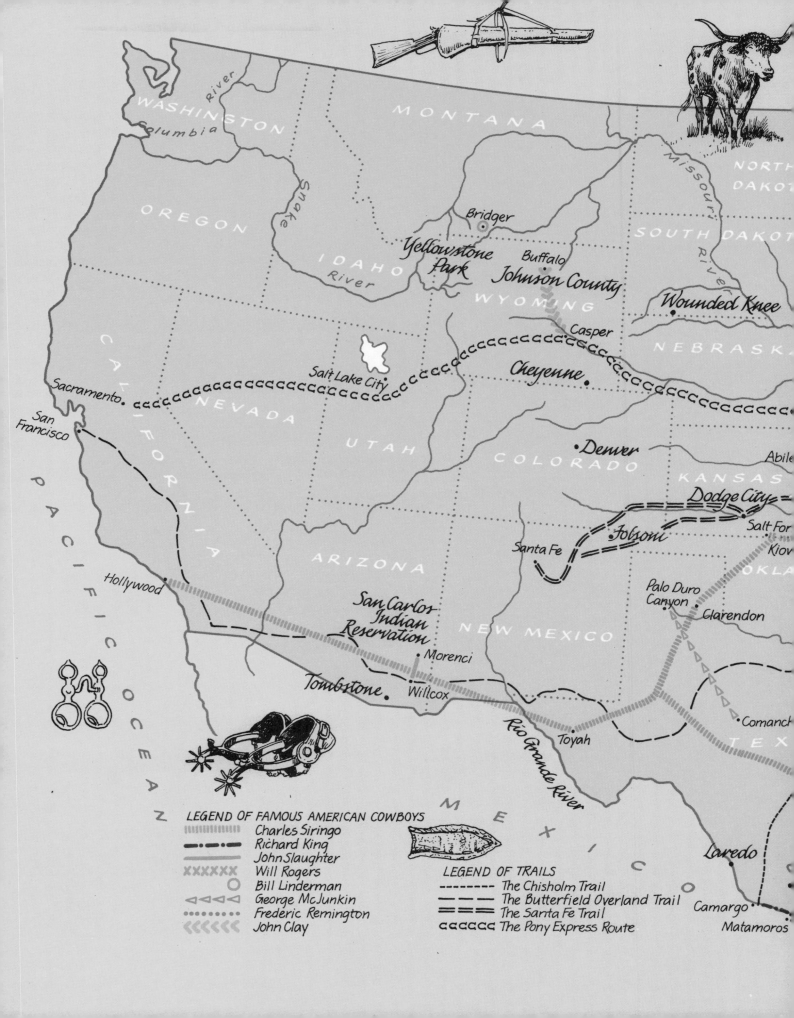

WASHINGTON

Columbia River

OREGON

IDAHO

Snake River

MONTANA

NORTH DAKOTA

Bridger

Yellowstone Park

Johnson County

Buffalo

WYOMING

Casper

Cheyenne

SOUTH DAKOTA

Wounded Knee

NEBRASKA

Salt Lake City

NEVADA

Sacramento

San Francisco

CALIFORNIA

UTAH

COLORADO

Denver

KANSAS

Dodge City

Abile

Santa Fe

Folsom

Salt For

Kiova

ARIZONA

NEW MEXICO

Palo Duro Canyon

Clarendon

OKLA

Hollywood

San Carlos Indian Reservation

Morenci

PACIFIC OCEAN

Tombstone

Willcox

Rio Grande River

Toyah

Comanch

TEXAS

MEXICO

Laredo

Camargo

Matamoros

LEGEND OF FAMOUS AMERICAN COWBOYS

.... Charles Siringo
—·—·— Richard King
———— John Slaughter
xxxxxx Will Rogers
O Bill Linderman
◁◁◁◁ George McJunkin
•••••• Frederic Remington
«««««« John Clay

LEGEND OF TRAILS

- - - - The Chisholm Trail
———— The Butterfield Overland Trail
≡≡≡ The Santa Fe Trail
ccccc The Pony Express Route